MAKE MONEY FROM HOME

START THE RIGHT HOME BUSINESS & FIND YOUR FIRST PAYING CUSTOMERS

SALLY MILLER

CONTENTS

Free Bonus   iii

Copyright   iv

1. Introduction   1
2. Getting Started   4
3. Kate's Success Story   13
4. Set Yourself Up For Success   17
5. Julie's Success Story   26
6. Build A Business Around You   29
7. Stephanie Donahue's Success Story   38
8. Find Your Business Idea   43
9. Pauline's Success Story   52
10. Make Your Business Stand Out   57
11. Clare's Success Story   65
12. Make Sure Your Idea Will Fly   70
13. Kendra's Success Story   83
14. Organize The Legal Stuff   88
15. Grow Your Business   96
16. Stephanie Johnson's Success Story   107
17. Build A Profitable Business   112
18. Conclusion   117

Notes   121

About Sally Miller   122

FREE BONUS

As a thank-you for buying my book, I have created a bonus area to help you on your journey. The bonus area has a growing list of resources that will help you:

> Finally stop dreaming and start earning money doing what you love.
> Discover proven strategies to build your five- or six-figure home business.
> Get a step-by-step guide that shows you exactly how to go from zero to your first $1000.

Plus, you will receive an invitation to join Sally's private Facebook group for more free training and support.

Download your bonus resources at:
sallyannmiller.com/bonus

1

INTRODUCTION

"Your work is going to fill a large part of your life, and the only way to be truly satisfied is to do what you believe is great work. And the only way to do great work is to love what you do."

— *Steve Jobs*

A re you ready to start a home business that fits you and your life? Do you want to get paid to do work you love? Are you struggling to decide whether to start a blog, write a book, become a coach, or offer freelancing services?

If so, you've come to the right place. This book is for anyone who is searching for the perfect business idea. It's also for people who want to build a home business that doesn't suck up all their time.

In this book, I walk you through a step-by-step process to create the best business for you. This isn't a one-size-fits-all solution. Each of us has a unique set of skills, experiences, and interests. The key to creating a successful business is leveraging what makes you special.

You want to stop copying other people and instead tap into your unique strengths. Focus on what you do best and do the work that you are uniquely designed to do.

This book teaches you how. It also shows you how to run your business so that it doesn't take over your life. Many people will say you have to hustle your way to success. I disagree. With solid systems and a commitment to following through, you can build a profitable business working fewer than 15 hours a week.

I know what it's like to have a burning desire to start a home business but no time to get it done. I'm a stay-at-home mom with two young children. I created my business while staying home with a baby and preschooler. I work between 15 and 20 hours each week—sometimes much less.

It *is* possible to build a profitable business and have time for all the other amazing things in your life. When you follow the steps in this book, you will find the prefect business idea and test it. You will then launch your business and create a solid foundation for growth.

Building a fulfilling and profitable business doesn't have to be difficult. In fact, the steps described in this book are quite simple. But don't be deceived. While you don't need a sophisticated business model, large team, or complex systems to create a six-figure business, you do need to commit to the process.

On your journey, you will face challenges and experience self-doubt. Your first idea will not yield the results you expect. Technology will break. People will criticize you. This is all part of the process. You must believe in your ability to create the business and life you want.

I know you have what it takes. So, I invite you to commit right now to following through with every step in this book.

Do this and by the time you've reached the final chapter—and followed the action steps—you will have designed a business and life you love. And whenever you find yourself doubting whether you can do this, check out the success stories. These are people just like you who have overcome the obstacles to create their ideal businesses. They have already done this. You can too.

2

GETTING STARTED

Now that you understand who the book is for (you!) and have had a brief introduction to the process, it's time to get started.

This book teaches you how to move through the iterative process of finding an idea, testing it, and building your business foundation. It also shows you how to implement simple but powerful systems to grow your business faster. These are the same tools I use in my business.

My goal is to help you find a business idea that's right for you and land your first paying customers. If you're prepared to embrace this process and take repeated action, then I guarantee you'll start a home business that's fulfilling and profitable.

But before we dive in, there are some extra steps I want you to take. These simple activities will ensure you get the most out of this book and achieve your goals much faster than you thought possible. There are three steps:

1. Commit to the process

2. Determine your why

3. Be accountable

At the end of this chapter, you'll find some action steps which will guide you through all three.

Step 1: Commit to the Process

Results come from action. It's not enough to read this book and set goals without implementing what you're learning. I want you to commit to following through with the action steps in this book.

Through the years, I've met many aspiring business owners. Most start out enthusiastic. They have ideas and are confident they will attain their goals. But along the way they encounter obstacles. Perhaps they struggle with technology, or their first business offering isn't well received.

This is normal. And I guarantee it will happen to you. Yet, obstacles don't have to be a reason to quit. Instead, they can be opportunities to learn. By experimenting, you will discover what works and what doesn't. You will refine your idea and over time you will create the perfect business for you.

So, make a pledge right now to keep working on your business no matter what. Commit to following all the action steps in this book. Even if you doubt whether an exercise will work for you, do it anyway. Stay curious, be open to possibility, and above all else keep moving forward. Do these things and you'll see far bigger results than ever before.

I recommend you block out time on your calendar to read this book and follow the action steps. Then share your commitment with someone. Do this and set yourself up for success from the start.

Step 2: Determine Your Why

When building a business, connecting with your why is one of the most powerful tools you can master. Your why is the reason you're pursuing your goal. The bigger your goal, the deeper your reasons need to be.

In the action steps, I ask you to identify your motivations for starting a home business. I also recommend you keep your motivations somewhere you can easily reference them.

Dig deep and be honest with yourself. Why do you *really* want to achieve this goal? For example, my motivations include:

* Earn an income from home so I can spend more time with my kids.

* Be a role model to my kids and other people who want to start a home business.

* Feel successful in a role outside of my family.

* Stop "wasting" my talents and start building a legacy.

* Live to my full potential and discover how much value I can create in the world.

Make sure you review your list of motivations every time fear or doubt threaten to surface. This will help you keep moving when you're feeling overwhelmed or want to give up.

Step 3: Be Accountable

Once you've set an intention to follow through with the steps in this book and have identified the reasons why this is important to you, it's time to address one of the biggest struggles all home business owners face. And that's staying consistent. When faced with technology problems, or when you're not seeing results fast enough, it's too easy to give up.

One answer to this problem is to create an accountability system. You need to find a way to hold yourself accountable for following through. When you work from home you enjoy the freedom to work when, where, and how you want. But this also means you have one big disadvantage over corporate employees. You don't have external accountability.

Accountability systems keep you from giving up when the going gets tough. Having one or more people to hold you accountable increases the likelihood of following through and creating the home business you want.

Now, some people don't require an external accountability system. Such people always keep their promises to themselves. They know that when they make a commitment, they will follow through no matter what.

> *Holding yourself accountable is a learnable skill. And it's one you need to develop. Every time you keep a commitment to yourself, you build self-belief. As your self-belief increases, your capacity to succeed also grows.*

However, even highly successful people can benefit from external accountability. In 2018, I interviewed 17 six- and seven-figure bloggers. I asked them what habits were key to their success. One of the biggest secrets they shared was the importance of creating systems to help you follow through.

Systems are key to making consistent progress toward your big goals. In chapter four, we talk more about systems. I share three simple but powerful systems that will help you build your home business much faster.

But there's one system you need to set up now, one that I personally find most effective. You need accountability. Having an accountability system is straightforward and yet incredibly effective when you compare it to passively reading a book or taking an online course. We are much more likely to follow through when we have an account-ability system.

When picking an accountability system, you have several options. We all respond better to different types of accountability. So, don't be afraid to experiment. Below are some ideas for you to consider.

Write Out Your Commitment

At the start of this chapter I asked you to commit to your business. This is the first step in building your self-belief. The second step is to follow through on your pledge. You must take the required action to keep your promise.

Remember, holding yourself accountable—and not relying on external accountability—is a learnable skill. To help you develop this skill, I suggest you write out your commitment and place it some-where visible. This could be in your workspace, by your bed, or next to the bathroom mirror. Make sure you have a constant reminder of your promise.

Some of my clients rewrite their commitment in their journal. They do this every day and it acts as a tangible reminder of what they've pledged to do.

As you take steps to fulfill your promise, you will build self-reliance. You will learn you can trust yourself. You will become bolder in your business and life.

Find an Accountability Partner

Now, you may still feel like you want some external accountability. Perhaps you've previously failed to stick to a new habit, and you doubt your ability to follow through on your own. This is normal. Please don't beat yourself up or judge yourself based on your past.

> *There's nothing wrong with seeking external accountability. It can be a helpful tool. However, you shouldn't rely on it. Always commit to building your self-belief. Know that you can do this on your own.*

One way to get external accountability is to find an accountability partner, someone who shares similar goals so you can understand each other's challenges. Meet regularly with your partner to report progress and brainstorm solutions to problems. To find a suitable partner, ask in online communities or reach out to a friend who has similar goals.

How and when you meet with your accountability partner is up to you. I have tried various methods, and all have been helpful. For example, I've had a daily accountability partner. We would check in with each other every morning by phone. This was extremely effective, but it does take discipline. You need to keep the phone calls short (less than 10 minutes) so you don't use up too much of your valuable time.

I've also had a weekly accountability partner. We exchanged emails at the start of every week and met on the phone for a longer call once a month. Pick the method that best fits your schedule. And when you meet with your partner, make sure you have a clear agenda. Here's an example agenda you can use:

1. Share your priorities or next steps for the current day or week.

2. Report progress against priorities for the previous day or week.

3. Describe any current challenges.

Join a Mastermind Group

Another option is to join a mastermind group. The group meets virtually or in person to help each other reach their goals. You can join a paid or unpaid mastermind.

The advantages of masterminds go way beyond accountability. In fact, their main function is so that members can receive input and support from their peers. The idea is that many minds are better than one.

As with accountability partners, you can start your own mastermind group by asking in online communities. For your mastermind calls, make sure you follow an agreed upon structure to keep everyone focused.

For example, you might start by going around the group and asking each person to briefly describe one win or achievement since you last met. Then, give each member a set amount of time in the hot seat. During that time, they present one challenge to the group and everyone helps them brainstorm solutions.

Share Your Goal

One final option to consider is sharing your goal (either with someone close to you or publicly).

For example, some people publish their monthly income reports on their blog or to their email list. This acts as a form of public accountability, motivating them to share strong performance each month.

You could also share on social media or inside a private community. If you don't want to share publicly, consider telling a close friend or spouse about your goals.

Action Steps

It's time to take your first action. At the end of each chapter, I include action steps to encourage you to follow through and start building your home business. You can also download a workbook with all the action steps here: **sallyannmiller.com/bonus**

1. Open your calendar right now and block out time to complete this book and act on it. This may be three or four hours every Sunday afternoon, or it may be 30 minutes every weekday. The amount of time or when you do it isn't important. What matters is that you take repeated action.

2. Next, think about why you're reading this book. What do you want to achieve over the next three to six months? Come up with two or three specific outcomes you want to achieve and write them down.

3. Share your answers to the previous question with someone close to you, a relevant Facebook community or Mastermind group. You can write something like this:

"I commit to completing this program and as a result I will achieve..."

4. Now, you want to determine your "why." Start by visualizing your goal. Imagine your future self as if you've already achieved all the specific outcomes listed in the previous step. Ask yourself the following questions:

i. Why is this goal important to me?

ii. What is at stake if I don't reach my goal?

iii. How will my life change if I do reach my goal?

Write down everything that comes to mind (you can always discard ideas later). Aim to identify at least five key motivations for starting your home business.

5. Next, prioritize your motivations in order of most important to least. Review your list of motivations and ask yourself these questions:

i. Which ones touch you the deepest?

ii. Which do you connect with most emotionally?

In your notebook, list your motivations in order from highest to lowest. Discard any motivations that you don't connect deeply with.

6. Once you're clear about why having a home business is important to you, you need to stay connected both emotionally and intellectually with your motivations. You need to understand and feel what is at stake. Place your goal motivations where you'll see them every day —such as on your desk, hanging on the wall, or set a notification on your phone.

7. Finally, review the accountability systems discussed in this chapter and pick at least one to try. They are: write out your commitment, find an accountability partner, join a mastermind group, share your goal. Implement your accountability system right now. For example, if you think an accountability partner will help you, reach out to a friend or ask in an online community for someone to partner with.

◆◆◆

Did you complete the above steps? Well done! By now you should have marked some time on your calendar to work through the steps in this book, identified your why, and implemented your accountability system.

Ready for some inspiration? Throughout this book, you'll meet people who have been where you are and worked through the process to create a profitable, fulfilling home business.

Now, I'd like to share Kate's story. Kate followed all three of the steps discussed in chapter two. She committed to the process and had a powerful reason to work from home—to spend time with her young children.

3

KATE'S SUCCESS STORY

Earning $1,600 in Her First Full Month as a Freelance Writer

This is Kate Burnett's story. Kate has a gift for words and always wanted to make money writing, but she worried this would mean low pay and long hours. When I first met Kate, I immediately felt a connection. We have a lot in common. We both love writing, are introverts (INFJs) and we're determined to stay home with our kids.

Kate wanted a business that gave her the freedom to be present with her family. Her love of writing led her to start a freelance writing business.

I find Kate's story inspiring for so many reasons, but what I love most is how she overcame her doubts and found the courage to call herself a writer. Here are some of Kate's highlights. During our time together, Kate:

* Created two websites in just five days.

* Overcame her fear of putting herself out there by declaring "I am a writer."

* Landed four freelancing clients (who all wanted to keep working with her).

* Earned $2,300 AUD (approximately $1,600 USD) in her first full month as a freelance writer.

You can find out more about Kate on her website: wordartistry.com.au

Can you tell us a bit about yourself and your business?

I've always had a passion for words. My earliest memories are filled with books, my father's made-up bedtime stories and notepads with chunky, childish handwriting.

Growing up in a chaotic environment, stories of other peoples' lives were my haven—my window into another world. It should have been obvious, but it took me 20-odd years of trying various jobs and becoming a mother to give myself permission to follow my dreams.

Why did you decide to start this business?

Children have a way of changing everything. Mostly, they changed my priorities. I was done dealing with petty office politics and sacrificing my values for the sake of somebody else's profit. I'd spent so much of my life helping other people achieve their goals and reached a point where I knew I needed to push past the fear and make my dream a reality if I wanted to live a fulfilled life.

But more than anything, I didn't want my kids to eat breakfast, lunch, and dinner at a long-hours daycare facility (which would also reduce my take-home pay to virtually nothing). I was determined to find a way to create a job that I loved while still being able to spend time with the people who mattered the most.

By creating a business that aligned with my values and made a difference in the world, I would also show my children that it *is* okay to follow your dreams and do what you love in life. Leaving that legacy to my children keeps me motivated to stay on track.

Was there anything holding you back from starting your business?

Yes! Mostly my belief that writers are "starving artists" and online entrepreneurs are slaves to their businesses, clocking unsustainable hours while putting their family on the back burner. I didn't believe I could make money writing.

Setting up a website was also challenging. I was torn between two career paths—blogging and freelance writing.

I got so stuck trying to figure out whether to start a blog or a freelance writing business, as well as who my target audience was, that I ended up taking a break from that decision-making process. I signed up for a blog building bootcamp that provided the shove (via a deadline) I needed to get unstuck.

I built two websites (blog and freelance writing) in five days. In the process of building both websites, the niche for my blog became obvious.

Then, with Sally's guidance, I decided to relax into freelance writing and let myself discover the direction I preferred through trying different styles.

How did you find your first freelancing clients?

I found my first two clients via Airtasker, an Australian online task bidding site, similar to Task Rabbit or Fiverr. My other two clients came about after I built the courage to tell people I'm a freelance writer.

A friend's sister owned a PR firm and offered to connect us which turned into a freelance job offer. Another friend became a client. Starting your own business is hard, but I think the toughest part is putting yourself out there and declaring "I am a writer."

In my first full month of freelance writing, I earned around $2,300 AUD (approximately $1,600 USD).

I haven't proactively sought further work, but most of my original clients have returned with more opportunities. So, I must be doing something right!

What are you looking forward to over the next year?

I'm really looking forward to seeing where this takes me. I'd like to grow my writing business at a pace that's sustainable for me and my family while also having fun on the journey.

Thanks to Sally's coaching, I now believe this is possible. I *can* have a profitable business that fits around my family life.

Like Kate, you might be feeling inspired with a few possibilities in your mind. Don't worry—this is a common part of the process, especially in the beginning. As you work through the action steps in the following chapters, you'll get clearer about which idea best matches your dreams and values and how to test that idea. Coming up next, I'll introduce you to the systems you'll need to succeed in your home business.

4

SET YOURSELF UP FOR SUCCESS

In the second chapter, you worked through the three steps of committing to the process, determining your why and finding accountability. A new home business needs a solid foundation in order to succeed. In this chapter, you'll learn how to set up systems to create a thriving home business.

What is the Home Biz Planner?

The Home Biz Planner is a set of tools I use in my business to make four to five figures a month, working 15 to 20 hours a week.

It incorporates three components:

1. Success Tracker

2. Weekly Priorities

3. 1-Page Home Biz Plan

Together, these tools will help you gain clarity, stay focused, make better decisions, and get results much faster than you thought possible.

You can find the link to download the *Home Biz Planner* here:

sallyannmiller.com/bonus

There are two versions of the planner. An Excel version (if you prefer to work on your computer) and a PDF version (if you prefer pen and paper).

Take a moment to look at the *Home Biz Planner* and familiarize yourself with the layout. I'll start by introducing the Success Tracker. This tool is the easiest to use, and most people find it's a lot of fun!

The purpose of the Success Tracker is to select one main goal for your home business, then track your progress toward your goal and celebrate your wins along the way.

Pick Your Success Track

Before I show you the tracker, you need to make a decision. I want you to pick a success track (don't worry, you can change your mind and switch tracks at any time). There are four success tracks, each one corresponding to a big goal. You want to select the goal which is most important to you right now.

Look back on your answers from the second chapter. Why are you starting a home business? Is it for the income (Money Track)? Or is it to make a big impact (Subscriber or Book Sales Track)? Perhaps you want to work one-on-one with clients but you don't have a specific income goal (Client Track).

Your track can change over time. You can even select more than one track. For example, I began by focusing on income but now my priorities are book sales and number of clients.

Here are the four tracks and the corresponding goals:

1. Money Track - earn your first $100,000

2. Subscriber Track - get your first 10,000 email subscribers

3. Client Track - work with your first 100 clients

4. Book Sales Track - sell your first 100,000 books

Note: These are lifetime goals. We're not talking about earning $100K in your first year of business. Instead, if you select the money track, then your goal is to earn your first $100,000 whether that takes six months or six years.

I picked these specific goals for several reasons. Once you achieve them, you will have a sustainable business. They are a stretch for new and early business owners but also achievable (we're not talking about earning seven figures here!) They can also be broken down into smaller goals so that you can easily measure your progress.

Also, please don't feel constrained by these tracks. Once you understand how the Success Tracker works, you can adapt it to fit you and your needs. For example, you may want to pick more than one track, or you may come up with a different main goal (other than money, subscribers, clients, or sales).

The key is to select one big, measurable goal, then break it down into smaller goals. The Success Tracker helps you do this by dividing each goal into a series of milestones. For example, the milestones in the Money Track are:

Milestone 1: $1

Milestone 2: $25

Milestone 3: $50

Milestone 4: $100

Milestone 5: $250

Milestone 6: $500

Milestone 7: $1,000

Milestone 8: $2,000

Milestone 9: $4,000

Milestone 10: $8,000

Milestone 11: $16,000

Milestone 12: $32,000

Milestone 13: $64,000

Milestone 14: $100,000

I talk more about how to use the Success Tracker in chapter seventeen. For now, all you need to do is familiarize yourself with the tool and select your success track.

Focus On What Matters

So, you have seen how the Success Tracker is set up. Next, I want to talk about planning your time. The second tool inside the *Home Biz Planner* is the Weekly Priorities. You can use this tool to set your priorities each week and month.

A core theme throughout this book is building a business without working long hours. And to do this you need to be extremely focused.

Most people you follow online don't have the responsibilities you have. They don't have kids or a full-time job or a relative to care for. They *can* spend 40 or more hours on their business each week. And most of them do. They have the time to experiment with new tactics, send out hundreds of sales emails, or play around with the latest technology.

You can't spend hours building a business and testing hundreds of ideas. You have a family or another responsibility. You need results fast. You need to be deliberate about what you do.

> *You need to have one main goal and focus only on the tasks that bring you closest to your goal.*

I see too many struggling business owners chasing trends. Experts urging you to jump on the latest new thing. Chatter about non-stop hustle and throwing spaghetti at the wall. It's exhausting. And confusing. And—in my opinion—not the fastest path to success.

Luckily there's another way to build your business. And throughout this book, I'm going to teach you so that you can build a successful business without missing out on family time. Next, we explore a system that will help you be more intentional about the tasks you choose to focus on.

How To Use The Weekly Priorities

Now, I'm going to walk you through the Weekly Priorities. This is the second tool in the Home Biz Planner. The Weekly Priorities is a single page where you can capture your tasks for the current month. The following is an overview of the sections inside the Weekly Priorities.

At the top of the page there's a space to enter the milestone you're currently working on. This is the next red milestone on your Success Tracker. For example, if you're following the Money Track and have earned $780 so far, then your next milestone would be $1,000.

Beneath the header, there's a space to set your priorities at the start of each week. And on the right, you can record your wins and struggles at the end of each week. Below is a snapshot of the Weekly Priorities.

In the action steps, I ask you to put a weekly appointment on your calendar to set your priorities. For example, you may want to do this every Sunday night or Monday morning.

When you set your priorities for the upcoming week, always make sure each task relates directly to your big goal. If you're not sure what you should be focusing on, ask yourself this question:

"What tasks will move me closer to achieving my next milestone?"

If a task is not important to your goal, then consider not doing it. Most people do far too many things in their business that have little or no impact on their success. When you only have a few hours to spend on your business, you want to make sure those hours make a difference.

As with all my tools, once you understand how the Weekly Priorities work, feel free to adapt it to suit you. For example, I handwrite my weekly tasks in my planner. I assign every task to a specific date and time. I like to work with pen and paper and know exactly when I'm going to get the work done.

Do what works best for you. The key is to set tasks at the start of each planning period and always make sure your priorities link directly to your next milestone or goal.

Create Your 1-Page Home Biz Plan

The third and final tool inside the *Home Biz Planner* is the 1-Page Home Biz Plan. Now, don't expect to fill out your 1-Page Home Biz Plan just yet. In the rest of this book, I will show you exactly how to complete the 1-Page Home Biz Plan.

Right now, I want to give you an overview of the tool so you understand why it's important and how it will help you stay focused in your business. The 1-Page Home Biz Plan does three things:

1. Identifies who your business is for, what you do, and why you're different from your competitors.

2. Shows the key activities in your business.

3. Records which metrics you use to measure your business progress.

By capturing all this information in a single page, you can see how the various parts of your business fit together. A good plan should be cohesive. There should be a clear flow from one section to the next.

There are many reasons why the 1-Page Home Biz Plan is an important tool in your business. First, it gives you clarity. You capture the important components of your business in one place. You can print your 1-Page Home Biz Plan and place it somewhere you can easily refer to.

Second, it helps you stay focused. The plan gives you a point of reference when deciding what to do next. If a new opportunity doesn't fit with your high-level business strategy, then you may want to pass on it.

Last, it saves you time by helping you do more of what works—not what isn't working. The metrics section of the 1-Page Home Biz Plan reminds you of the important data in your business so you can focus on achieving your main goal.

Action Steps

Now that you've had a look at the Home Biz Planner, it's time to take action. Work through the steps below. You can download both the *Home Biz Planner* and a workbook with all the action steps here:

sallyannmiller.com/bonus

> *Don't feel like you have to rush through these steps. Take your time and trust the process.*

1. Look back on the motivations you wrote down in chapter two. Think about why you're starting a home business. It may be for the income (Money Track), to make a big impact (Subscriber or Book Sales Track) or perhaps to work one-on-one with clients (Client Track).

2. Select the Success Track that best fits you and your business.

* Money Track - earn your first $100,000

* Subscriber Track - get your first 10,000 email subscribers

* Client Track - work with your first 100 clients

* Book Sales Track - sell your first 100,000 books

Remember, your track can change over time. So, don't worry about being locked in to one track. Focus on what's most important to you right now.

3. Determine your planning period. This defines how often you want to set your priorities. For example: daily, weekly or monthly. If you're not sure, start with weekly and see how it goes.

4. Next, put a recurring appointment on your calendar to remind you to set your priorities at the start of each planning period. For example, if you're planning weekly, then you might put a recurring appointment on your calendar to set your priorities every Monday morning.

5. Finally, decide where you want to track your priorities. You could use the Excel version of the Weekly Priorities sheet inside the Home Biz Planner. Or you could print the PDF version and handwrite your priorities. You can also use a desk calendar. If you do this, make sure you write your next milestone somewhere you can easily refer to it.

Every time you set your weekly priorities, ask yourself this question:

"What tasks will move me closer to achieving my next milestone?"

This simple question will help you focus on the most important tasks in your business.

◆◆◆

Congratulations! You've just done the work to set up tracking systems you'll need to create a successful home business. If you're feeling a little overwhelmed at this point, just relax and breathe. This is a normal part of the process.

Our brain often views a new thing as potentially dangerous and will work overtime to stop you from doing it. This is one of the reasons it's important to keep your why (from chapter two) in front of you every day.

Staying focused on your reasons for starting a home business (that you love!) will keep you moving forward, even when your brain is trying to stop you.

Now, I'd like to share Julie's story with you. Julie struggled to get clarity in her business. By really digging into her why, selecting one big goal and putting a plan in place, Julie was able to go from uncertainty in her business to thriving.

5

JULIE'S SUCCESS STORY

Growing an Author Business as a Podcast Guest

Julie Schooler is an author, blogger, and speaker. When we started working together, she had already published seven books. However, Julie struggled to grow her business as an author. She wanted to build her tribe, sell more books, and earn a real income from her work.

Here are some of Julie's highlights:

* Julie overcame her fear of "niching down" and came up with a clear message that excited her and appealed to her ideal customers.

* Moved through her fear of rejection and took massive action by sending her first 20 pitches to podcasters.

* Landed three podcast interviews and counting, which helped grow her audience, spread her message, and sell more books.

* Beat procrastination and finally wrote the first draft of her next book in less than a month.

You can find out more about Julie and her books on her website: julieschooler.com.

Was there anything specific you were struggling with when you started out?

I struggled with two main things. The first involved getting clear about who my ideal customer was. I worried about choosing a niche because: 1) I might get bored, 2) A narrow niche might void all the books I'd already written and 3) I didn't want to step on anyone's toes by "invading their niche."

Of course, now I realize these thoughts were limiting beliefs. Sally helped me by nailing down my message: "Rediscover Your Sparkle." It felt so good to have a clear message that I believed in—something that resonated with my readers.

My second challenge was how to promote myself and my books without feeling like I might be constantly rejected. I decided to start doing podcast interviews. I planned to appear as a guest on podcasts where my potential customers hung out.

We decided to make pitching to podcasts into a game. I made it a habit to send two pitches each week for a year. I would "win" (i.e. not feel rejected) if I got featured on 10 or more podcasts over the course of the year.

Well so far, I have three YES's and a handful of maybes from less than 20 pitches! I'm thrilled to be seeing results so quickly.

What's the most challenging part of growing your business and how are you overcoming it?

There are still many challenging parts. But the biggest is deciding what to focus on with limited hours in the day. There's so much to do —writing, marketing, social media, the latest binge watch sensation, making good money from my books, growing a tribe.

Knowing that I love creating stuff is helping me focus on the important tasks in my business. The more focused work I put in, the better my results seem to be.

My next big project is a book called *Rediscover Your Sparkle*. The eBook version will be available for free on all online platforms so I can get more readers and customers who want to read my blog, listen to my podcast interviews, and buy my books.

It's a work in progress. But I know I'm on the right track and this is giving me the motivation to keep moving forward.

What are you most looking forward to over the next year?

After decluttering my own house in March, I'm looking forward to writing book number nine. This one will be about decluttering, which I've been talking about forever.

Also, being on 10-plus podcast interviews is exciting. I look forward to seeing the impact *Rediscover Your Sparkle* will have on my business.

I love what I do now.

Julie's story is inspiring. Through committing to one thing (being interviewed as a podcast guest) she was able to grow her audience and sell more books. Of course, appearing on podcasts is only one of thousands of ways to market your business online.

Just as we've discussed in this chapter, the key to building your tribe is to focus on the one big goal that works for you. Keep up with activities that move you closer to your goal every single week.

Next up, we dig a little deeper and explore how to find the right business idea based on who you are and what you want. Plus, I'll walk you through how to find your passion.

6

BUILD A BUSINESS AROUND YOU

In chapter four, we looked at the *Home Biz Planner* and set up systems for your success. In this chapter, you'll find your first business idea based on who you are and what you want. Or, if you already have a business, you will know you've selected the right one. Here's what you will learn:

1. How to find your business idea

2. Why passion is important

3. How to find your passion (even if you have no interests or too many interests)

How To Find Your Business Idea

Okay, are you ready to find (or validate) your home business idea? Even if you already know what you want to do or have an existing business, I encourage you to work through the steps in this chapter.

The approach we're going to take to finding your business idea is two-fold. First, you're going to seek to build a business around you. I will ask you to think about what makes you special and what kind of business you want.

Second, you will make sure you can make money from your business idea. There's no point going too deep and then discovering there's no market for your idea.

The work you do now will help you create a business that feels meaningful, fits the lifestyle you want, and generates a positive income for you.

In the first part of this process, you will get to know who you are. I want you to dig deep and understand what makes you special. I will ask you to explore your skills, experiences, and characteristics. The more you can infuse your business with YOU, the happier you will be and the more people (customers) will respond to your work.

In short, I want you to build a business you are passionate about—a business which also makes money.

Why Passion Is Important

"Passion is energy. Feel the power that comes from focusing on what excites you."

— OPRAH WINFREY

In 2018, I took my daughter and her friends to see the latest Peter Rabbit movie. It was her seventh birthday. The girls had a wild time eating popcorn and gossiping. I think they enjoyed the movie, too.

I didn't eat popcorn or gossip. But I did take something away from the movie. Something important. What moved me was Bea's character.

Bea is the female lead in the movie. She lives in a cottage nestled in the English countryside. Bea loves to paint. She loses herself in her art. Painting is her passion.

But here's the thing: Bea's art is horrible except for her rabbit illustrations. Her detailed creations bring the rabbits to life.

Two things struck me about Bea's character. First, she's pursuing her passion regardless of what others think. Second, her passion eventually leads to remarkable results.

Bea is, of course, loosely based on Beatrix Potter, creator of Peter Rabbit. Beatrix Potter wrote and illustrated dozens of books that have charmed generations. She became a wealthy woman. When she passed away, she left fifteen farms and over four thousand acres of land to the National Trust.

Her passion led her to build a profitable business and leave a legacy in the world. Pursuing your passion is about using your gifts. Spending time in your sweet spot. Doing more of what you're designed to do.

How To Find Your Passion

Now, you may be thinking you don't have a passion. Or, if you're like me, you have many interests and don't want to be pinned down to just one thing.

That's where knowing yourself comes in. In this chapter, I walk you through a process to get to know who you are and what makes you special. I ask you to identify the skills, experiences, and knowledge you have gained throughout your life. I also ask you a series of questions to help you dig deep and understand what is most important to you.

This works for any kind of business, whether you want to make money blogging, freelancing, coaching, writing, or even selling physical products.

Then, you will review all your answers and select ten or more possible business topics. Your topic is the first of three components that make up your business idea. The other two components are your customers and offering. Here's a definition of all three:

Topic – This is the field or broad subject matter of your business. For example: health and nutrition, basketball, online business, cooking.

Customers – These are the people your business serves. For example: new dads, recent college graduates, people with celiac disease.

Offering – This is how you serve your customers. For example: an online course, a one-on-one coaching program, physical products.

In future chapters, you will narrow down to one business topic. You will also define the other two components of your business.

Design the Life You Want

Knowing what makes you special is one part of selecting the right business for you. The other part is understanding the lifestyle you want for yourself and your family.

The right home business offers the kind of life you want.

If you don't enjoy working one-on-one with people, then coaching may not be a good fit for you. Or if you're the kind of person who thrives on constant human connection, then you may struggle to build a business as an author.

So, do you have a clear picture of exactly what you want in your life? Where will you be two or three years from now? What will you be doing? How much money will you be earning? What big life dream(s) will you have achieved? What will your typical day look like? Will you have employees? Or will you work alone?

If you want to create a business that provides the lifestyle you want, you must answer these questions. Then, intentionally create a business that fits your future vision. The action steps at the end of this chapter will help you do this.

What's Your Definition Of Success?

We all want to succeed in life, but most people fail to take the time to figure out what success means to them. As a result, they end up trapped in a job or business they find draining or unfulfilling. For example, do you want a:

* Big business in which you employ hundreds or thousands of people and have transformed the lives of millions?

* Small business with no more than 100 employees?

* Micro business with zero or just a handful of employees/sub-contractors?

Each of these are different paths and involve making different decisions. As a reader of this book, I'm guessing you fall into the last category—though there's no reason why you can't start a micro business that eventually evolves into a small or even a big business.

Something else to consider is that your business or work is just one component of your life.

I'm passionate about helping people build a business that leaves space for the other amazing things in their life. To be truly successful, you must focus on more than money and recognition. Science backs up this point of view.

Psychologists believe we have an inner life and an outer life. Success in your outer life revolves around achievements, career, and money, as well as anything else you normally associate with success. Whereas, your inner life is about happiness, purpose, and connection.

It seems that most people talk about one or the other of these concepts, but it's my belief that you need to consider both at the same time.

The balance between the two is different for each person and can change throughout your life. But to be successful, you must honor outer achievements and inner happiness.

So, as you think about what success means to you, consider your inner happiness. What is it that matters most to you?

You won't want to build a home business that requires you to work around the clock if your goal is to spend more time with your kids or grandkids.

Business Vision Exercise

In the action steps below, I share a business vision exercise. This will help you answer the questions posed above.

I write my business vision at least once a year. As I meet goals and my life shifts, my vision for the future changes, but there are always recurring themes like my focus on doing work I love while enjoying quality time with my family.

It's important to review your future vision throughout the year. This will keep you on the right track. Completing the business vision exercise also gives you direction and motivation. It helps you stop doing the things that are unimportant and start doing what matters most to you.

Let's get started.

Action Steps

The best businesses reflect who you are and the work you're meant to do. So, we're going to start by getting to know who you are and what makes you special. In the downloadable workbook at sallyannmiller.com/bonus or in your journal, work through the following steps. Take your time to fully consider each question before answering. This is an important process, so don't rush.

1. Start by listing at least 20 things you're good at. Examples: Are you

good with numbers? Are you organized? Are you skilled at time management? Do you have a degree? Good with children? Confident public speaker? Know the Bible from front to back? Love to write?

Don't overthink it. Write anything and everything that comes to mind. If you are struggling to come up with 20 different skillsets, take a break and come back to it later. Ask friends and family for ideas.

2. When you're done with step one, circle five skillsets in your list that you identify with the most or have the most experience with.

3. Now, list experiences in your life which have had a big impact on you. For example: had a baby in the NICU, gone through a difficult divorce, lost a family member, been in a management or leadership position, had a child with a learning disability, completed an advanced degree.

4. Next to each of your life experiences, write out the wisdom you gained through that experience. If you went through a divorce, did you learn how to hire the best lawyer? Or did you learn how to emotionally cope with losing someone you loved? If you have held a leadership position, did you learn how to motivate your team? Did you learn how to interview for a promotion? Try to list five things you learned through each of your experiences.

5. Let's dig a little deeper. Ask yourself the following questions and write out your answers:

What do the people closest to you say about you? How do they describe you?

What comes easily to you that you love doing?

Which skills do you perform almost daily without really thinking about it?

What could you talk about for hours on end?

What do people say you excel in?

What is unique about you?

What did you want to be when you grew up?

What do people naturally come to you for help with?

What brings you the most joy in life?

Who are you most comfortable speaking to (e.g. women in their fifties)?

6. Now, review all your answers above and brainstorm at least 10 topics you could build a business around. Right now, I don't want you to worry about how your business makes money (e.g. courses, books, coaching, physical products, affiliate sales). Also, please don't stress too much over this—there's always more than one answer here. List ten or more potential topics.

Make sure each idea uses some of the skills, experiences, and knowledge you identified in the previous steps. If it doesn't come to you right away, give yourself some time to mull it over.

7. Now, find a quiet space and imagine how your life will look two years from now. Assume you are living your best possible life. Focus on what you are doing in your business. You can also imagine other areas of your life such as relationships, spirituality, and health. But remember this book is designed to help you create a home business you love.

Also, avoid thinking about how your current life doesn't match this ideal future. You may be tempted to think about how accomplishing goals has been difficult for you in the past, or about financial/time/social barriers that might limit your success. For the purpose of this exercise, imagine a brighter future in which your circumstances change just enough to bring your dreams to fruition.

Be as creative and imaginative as you want. Have fun!

8. Now write down your future vision in as much detail as possible. By writing it down, you make it real. This helps you move from the world of vague ideas to concrete possibilities. You also have a permanent record of what you want right now.

9. After writing down your future vision, take a break for a day or two. Then come back and reread it. Reflect on how it makes you feel.

Do you feel excited about this future?

Does it capture what you want most in life?

Does it scare you (at least a little)?

Are you doing more of the things you love and less of the things you don't?

Are you using your unique strengths?

Are you honoring your core values?

Feel free to go back and add or change details. Your future vision will evolve over time. What's important is that you have a direction to start moving toward right now—a future that both scares and excites you.

Fantastic! You're on your way to finding your home business idea. You may be tempted to jump ahead and pick one idea right now. Please don't succumb to this temptation.

If you want a business that has the best chance of succeeding, then trust the process and follow all the steps in this book.

If you're feeling overwhelmed by the number of business ideas you've generated, you're not alone. Please don't give in to the overwhelm. If you keep following the steps in this book, you will find the perfect business for you. Let me introduce you to Stephanie, who also struggled with too many ideas. Read on for her full story.

7

STEPHANIE DONAHUE'S SUCCESS STORY

From Overwhelm to a Growing Coaching Business

This is Stephanie Donahue's home business success story. When I first met Stephanie, she was juggling multiple jobs and feeling overwhelmed. During our time together, Stephanie discovered work she was passionate about and finally defeated the overwhelm.

Here are some of Stephanie's highlights:

* She discovered where her true passion[1] and purpose lay.

* Landed three coaching clients in one month.

* Overcame her self-doubt and found a new confidence in her role as a coach.

* Created systems that reduced her overwhelm and freed her to spend more time with family.

You can visit Stephanie's website at StephanieDonahue.co

Going Nowhere

The first thing that struck me about Stephanie was her huge and generous heart. Stephanie loved to help people and struggled to say no.

These are all incredible qualities, but they can lead to overwhelm. Here's what Stephanie told me when we first started working together:

> *"I get easily over-committed because I love to serve anyone who wants my help. I loved nursing when I was a nurse. When I started my health and wellness blog, I loved talking about healthy habits. Then, I realized bloggers were a more receptive audience so I put my heart into helping bloggers and loved that. Then, I started buying more expensive courses where I met with entrepreneurs of all backgrounds and found that I love helping all entrepreneurs. Now, for the last couple of months I have put my heart into helping my husband and business partner implement EOS/Rocket Fuel method for his business and I love that, too."*

Pursuing too many ideas is a common problem for people wanting to start a home business. When we first discover the world of online business, we are pulled in so many interesting directions.

But when we jump into multiple projects, we end up spreading ourselves too thin. It's impossible to achieve a big goal when we are busy chasing too many small goals.

The solution is to figure out what you want most, then focus your energies in that one direction. This is what Stephanie did. She threw herself into the discovery exercises I shared with her and quickly identified her true passion. She told me:

> *"I've been split in too many directions going nowhere. I need help to get the courage to focus on my ONE thing which right now is to become a paid coach. It truly is my passion!"*

In every conversation I had with Stephanie, we kept returning to the idea of coaching. It was obvious to both of us that Stephanie needed to explore the idea further.

Eliminating Overwhelm

Deciding to explore coaching was pivotal. But Stephanie still needed to figure out how to fit coaching into her already busy schedule.

Stephanie found value in two tools. The first was to focus on the few things that aligned with her biggest priorities. This meant eliminating tasks that weren't important, learning to say "no," and spending time doing the 20 percent of things that generated 80 percent of the results.

The second tool was implementing boundaries. One of Stephanie's greatest priorities was her family and spending time with her kids was important to her. Stephanie enforced some simple boundaries around her family and work time so she could give her kids more focused attention.

Here's what Stephanie told me:

> *"I've come to realize that I needed this program to learn to create boundaries. I also needed help to see the excess work I could cut out so that I can leave a legacy for my kids and spend more time educating them, learning about life through playing together, and helping them develop good character. I'm shifting my work hours to six to eight a.m. and one to five p.m. so that I'm on my A game with my kids at my best hours which is from eight a.m. to one p.m. These changes bring me joy and peace, knowing I'm on the right track to have an abundant life which includes a thriving business."*

Growing Her Confidence As A Coach

Stephanie learned to manage her time and felt less overwhelmed, but there was a second challenge. She began to doubt her value as a coach. Early on in our time together, she told me:

> *"I yearn to be a coach and feel like it is within my grasp, but I don't have enough value to offer yet or experience."*

I hear comments like this all the time. We all doubt whether we are good enough or know enough or have enough experience.

But this is fear talking, and it wasn't Stephanie's truth. She'd been supporting entrepreneurs for over a year and had helped her husband's business implement a new marketing system.

Stephanie had the experience and the skills to be an effective coach. She just needed to act in spite of the fear—which is what she did when she reached out to her network and started looking for coaching clients.[2] Within a month, Stephanie had three paying clients.

Here's what Stephanie told me about doing it scared:

> *"I learned so much about myself and my core identity through this journey. I feel that it has empowered me to embrace coaching whether I feel ready or not. I still feel that I do not have enough experience to be a business coach, but the results my clients are getting are debunking that false belief I've held. Thank you for the encouragement all this time!"*

As time went by, Stephanie's self-belief grew. Recently she sent me this message:

> *"I love coaching! I had my first call of the day this morning and it was awesome!"*

And a few days later:

"I feel like the coaching I have done lately has helped me gain confidence and find my voice!"

Stephanie's story highlights the power of doing the kind of work you're meant to do. When you're pursuing work you're passionate about, your fear becomes irrelevant. You know you're on the right path. This is how Stephanie explained it to me:

"You may know that I take a lot of courses and have a lot of mentors, but [working with you] was pivotal and a defining moment in my life to start doing what I am meant to do. Seeing the new glow in my clients is so rewarding that I can't even put a monetary value to it. I am filled with gratitude that I met you."

I hope you found Stephanie's story inspiring. By narrowing her focus, she proved that it's possible to move beyond feeling stuck and overwhelmed to creating a home business that suited her personality, skills, passion, and vision for the future. If you've completed the action steps, you should have identified a list of ten possible business topics. Coming up, you'll refine this list and select a business idea you can test in the real world.

8

FIND YOUR BUSINESS IDEA

O kay, it's time to pull everything together and pick your first business idea. In chapter six, you identified at least ten possible business topics. You also defined the kind of life you want.

In this chapter, you will choose one business topic and decide how you will make money from your business. If you haven't completed the action steps from chapter six, go ahead and do that now.

Already completed? Fantastic! You're ready to find your business idea.

A Word About Uncertainty

At this point, fear or doubt may be bubbling up. You might be thinking, "I can't do this," or, "Picking one idea will limit me too much," or, "None of my ideas are good enough."

If this is you, then stop. Take a deep breath and trust the process. There's no need to put pressure on yourself. Building a home business can be an exciting journey. Yes, there will be ups and downs, but following the steps in this book will give you the tools and insights to navigate the bumpy road.

Everything you've done up to this point is designed to increase your chances of success. And remember, starting the right home business is an iterative process. First, you pick an idea. Then, you test it. And finally, you refine or change your idea based on feedback. You keep iterating through this process until you have a business that's both profitable and fulfilling.

You're at the first stage in this process. You're about to select a business idea, then take the necessary steps toward building a business you love. You got this.

How To Make Money From Your Idea

Up until this point, we've focused on you. What makes you special and what kind of lifestyle you want. We haven't talked about *how* you will make money. Your goal is to make money from home, so you need a way to earn an income from your business topic.

You will need to do some preliminary research to see whether there's a market for each of the business topics you identified in chapter six. This research should only take five to ten minutes per topic.

> *For now, you simply need to answer the question: Are people already making money in this area?*

You may find it helpful to take note of how they are making money (e.g. selling services, affiliate sales, eBooks, courses, coaching, or physical products).

Below are some ways you can research your topics. There's no need to do your research in all these places. Pick one or two research methods that are most appropriate for you.

Research Using Amazon

With millions of products and customer reviews, Amazon is an excellent place to investigate a range of business ideas. Start by searching for books or other products on your topic and see if they are selling. Here's how to find sales data on Amazon:

1. Head over to Amazon.com and type a search term relating to your business topic into Amazon's search box.

2. Select four to six books or other products in your business topic. Try to find products with a lot of reviews.

3. View the Amazon product pages for the products you selected and find the overall sales ranking. You can find this by scrolling down the page to the Product Details area. Then look for the Amazon Best Sellers Rank. You will find one or more ranking numbers for the different product categories the item is listed in. For example, a book ranking might look like this:

#82,030 Paid in Kindle Store

#27 in Blogging (Kindle Store)

4. Finally, use the Jungle Scout Amazon Sales Estimator[1] to estimate the number of monthly sales for the product based on its ranking.

If items related to your topic have multiple sales per month, then other people are making money in this area.

Research With Udemy

Udemy is a platform where you can find online courses in just about any topic. To research your idea on Udemy, search for courses on your topic and see if they are selling.

You can't see how much the students paid (they may even have received the course for free). So, look for courses with a lot of enrollments and make sure they have a range of reviews spread over different date periods.

Research On Forums and Q&A Sites

Research sites like Reddit and Quora are great places to gather insights about the market in your topic. People tend to openly ask personal questions and give honest opinions on topics and products that are relevant to them.

Be on the lookout for discussions around actual products and services in your topic that people are buying.

Research Using Blogs

Many bloggers publish their income reports to share their journey and encourage others. Look for bloggers in the topic and see if any are reporting positive income. Also note how they are making money from their blog.

Ask Family And Friends

Finally, you can talk to people and learn what others think about your topic ideas. Be curious and listen for the types of products and services people are buying. Also, what blogs and websites they visit most often and why.

As you do your research, eliminate any business topics that have limited earning potential.

How To Select Your Business Idea

Once you've completed your research, rank your remaining topics according to which ones are the best fit for you. Remember, your main focus is starting a business that's both profitable and personally fulfilling.

In the action steps below, I provide a ranking matrix you can use to do this. The suggested criteria to rank your topics are:

1. Do you have existing skills and/or experience in this topic?

2. Would you enjoy learning more about this topic?

3. Can you bring something unique to this topic?

4. Do you feel connected to potential audiences in this topic?

5. Do you have existing contacts in this topic?

6. Do you have the necessary resources (money and time) for this topic?

7. Does this topic fit with your future vision?

These questions are designed to help you identify the topics that best fit you and your desired lifestyle.

Your Offering

The final step in this chapter is to pick one idea to run with (usually the topic with the highest ranking). Then, brainstorm at least one possible offering. An offering is how you make money from your business.

As with your research, there's no need to go into detail here. We will go much deeper into your offering(s) in future chapters. You may even change your offering later down the track. This is okay. Your goal right now is to select a business topic and make sure there's at least one way you can make money from it.

Below is a list of possible offerings. This list is not complete. It's intended to get you thinking about all the possible ways you can make money in your business.

Products

Crafted products such as jewelry, clothing, art, stationery

Manufactured products such as sporting goods, home décor, clothing, beauty items

Books

Apps and games

SaaS (Software-as-a-Service)

Music

Information products such as online courses, eBooks, membership sites

Other people's products (affiliate marketing)

Services

Coaching or consulting

Graphic design

Database management

Data entry

Bookkeeping

Accounting

Legal services

Researching

Transcription

Video creation/editing/uploading

Blog management

Social media management

Marketing services

Copywriting

Copyediting/developmental editing/proofreading

Event coordination

Customer service

Email management

Freelance writing

Website development

App development

Other people's services (affiliate marketing)

Advertising space, sponsored posts

Trust The Process

Before you jump into the action steps, one final word of caution. Finding the best business idea doesn't always happen the first time around. So please be patient and don't put too much pressure on yourself to get it right.

Remember, the process you're learning is iterative. That is, you need to first select an idea and test it. Then take the feedback (what worked and what didn't) and either refine your idea or pick a new one. The same formula can be followed for each business idea until you find the one that works best for you.

Trust the process and have fun. Building a home business doesn't have to be overwhelming.

Action Steps

1. Follow the steps outlined in the beginning of this chapter and research each of the 10 topics you outlined in chapter six.

2. Eliminate any topics in which there's no market (people aren't already paying for products or services) in the subject area.

3. Now, write down your new shortlist of business topics. Hopefully, you still have at least five.

4. Next, score your topics against the criteria you explored in the

previous steps. In other words, select the topic that best fits you and the life you want. Complete the matrix below by assigning a one to five rating against each question for each topic. Then, total the scores for each topic.

Scoring: 1 = strongly disagree, 2 = disagree, 3 = neutral, 4 = agree, 5 = strongly agree					
	TOPIC 1:	TOPIC 2:	TOPIC 3:	TOPIC 4:	TOPIC 5:
1. I have existing skills and/or experience in this topic.					
2. I would enjoy learning more about this topic.					
3. I can bring something unique to this topic.					
4. I feel connected to potential audiences on this topic.					
5. I have existing contacts in this topic.					
6. I have the necessary resources (money and time) for this topic.					
7. This topic fits with my future vision.					
TOTALS:					

Did one or more topics stand out? Are you surprised by the results? If you're feeling uncertain, I ask you to keep moving forward anyway. This system is designed to help you pick one or more business ideas that have the best chance of succeeding for you. Pick one winning topic (usually the highest scoring one) and move on.

5. Next, define one or two offerings for your winning topic. Your goal here is to decide how you want to serve your audience in the business topic. In your notebook, briefly describe the product (or service) you can offer. For example, if your topic is "online business," your offering might be:

A downloadable eBook or short course about how to start an online business ($27)

A video course on building an email list ($197)

A one-on-one coaching intensive to help people define their first online product ($497)

A premium group coaching program to help people get more customers online ($997)

A done-for-you search engine optimization service ($97/month)

A content writing and blog management service ($350/month)

A software solution or other product for online business owners ($47 - $497)

6. Finally, reflect on how your above answer makes you feel. Are you excited to deliver this offering? If not, repeat step five. You can either do this for the same subject area or one of your other top scoring topics. Keep brainstorming and writing out business ideas until you have a topic and an offering you feel excited about.

7. If you haven't already done so, download the *Home Biz Planner* at **sallyannmiller.com/bonus** and enter your Business Topic in the relevant space on the 1-Page Home Business Plan.

How did you do with the action steps? You have now researched your ten topics and selected one topic to move forward with. From there, you worked through how to choose an offering. Remember, don't get hung up on the details. We will refine your offering in future chapters.

Don't worry if you have no clue how to deliver the service or product. If you wait until you understand everything about how to run your business, you will never start. Take one step at a time and trust the process.

Next up, I'd like to introduce you to Pauline. Her story is a great example of the iterative process of testing business ideas to find one that suits you best.

9

PAULINE'S SUCCESS STORY

Signing Six Paying Clients in Three Months

T his is another success story from one of my clients. Pauline started out as a freelance writer and eventually found her purpose as a life coach. She started a life coaching business and signed her first six paying clients in three months.

I love Pauline's story because, just as we discovered in the previous chapter, it shows how finding the right business is rarely a straightforward process. Here are some of Pauline's highlights:

* Pauline landed a $500 freelance writing job (and got paid!) in her first month.

* Pivoted her business when she realized that freelancing wasn't the path for her.

* Discovered her true purpose as a life coach.

* Overcame her fear of selling and found a way to market herself that didn't feel icky.

* Signed her first six paying clients in a three-month period.

You can visit Pauline's website at: paulinecheungcoaching.com

Wanting To Have A Career And Be A Mom

When I first started working with Pauline, she was a full-time mom. She had already moved on from corporate life after her son was born and also closed her side business for health reasons.

While she loved being a mom, Pauline felt called to do something more in her life. But she didn't want to return to a hectic schedule and give up precious time with her son. There was a growing tension between her role as a mother and her need for meaningful work. Pauline couldn't figure out how to resolve this.

So, we set out to find work she could do from home. Work that would fulfill her desire for personal growth and provide the flexibility she valued. And, of course, an income.

Gaining Clarity By Taking Action

Pauline's first challenge was to uncover the right kind of work for her. She had many skills and ideas. Narrowing down her options to just one wasn't easy.

This is the kind of challenge I love. I believe work is most profitable and fulfilling when you pursue the activities you're uniquely designed to do. We all have a set of skills, experiences, and passions.[1] When you build a business around these, you discover the kind of work that's right for you.

But Pauline's problem was not having too few ideas. Instead, she had too many. How could she settle on one path? The answer was to pick one idea and go with it. Here's what Pauline said:

> *"I want to do something, but I'm struggling to nail down what that something should be, so the next best thing is to run with the most feasible idea and take it from there."*

Pauline initially felt drawn to freelance writing. She enjoyed organizing her thoughts on paper, and she knew she could hit the ground running and find out whether freelancing would fit around her home life.

Within a month of deciding to explore it, Pauline landed a $500 writing job. She was asked to create a 4,000-word blog post for an online marketer.

Pauline's writing rate worked out over 12 cents a word. This was an admirable rate for a new freelancer, and a million miles away from the low-paying jobs offered by content mills.

Pauline went ahead and completed the job, then celebrated her first paycheck. But then she faced her second challenge: She realized writing for someone else wasn't going to keep her motivated in the long-term. While there were many advantages to a freelance writing career, it wasn't the right path for her.

Instead of seeing this as a setback, Pauline understood this was a good thing. By taking action, she'd quickly discovered what didn't work for her and felt free to move on. She even got paid to make the discovery!

Finding Purpose As A Coach

Pauline decided to dig deeper, to get past her obvious skills and experience. She took time to uncover her true passions. What kind of work felt most purposeful and fulfilling? What would be profitable and fit around her role as a mom?

Pauline did a lot of research and self-exploration. As she did this, one idea kept rising to the surface. Her real dream was to coach people.

As we discussed her next steps, Pauline became excited about the future. Gradually her path forward became clear. Pauline told me:

> *"Thanks for doing your magic and helping me find the next step forward from this mass of information I've gathered."*

Signing Her First Six Paying Clients

But of course, deciding to become a coach didn't mean the hard work was over. In fact, reaching this conclusion was the start of another difficult journey.

New coaches are faced with many challenges. How do you pick a coaching niche? How much should you charge? And how do you find your first paying clients?

Pauline's biggest concern was how to sell her coaching services in a way that felt natural. Pauline loved coaching but felt uncomfortable with the thought of asking people to pay her. Here's what Pauline told me:

> *"I feel icky about selling. I don't think it's a fear, it's more of the icky feeing of having to sell, based on the way others tell me how to sell. Even the 'experts' who claim to teach non-icky selling, still come off too salesy. I somehow need to get to the bottom of this so I can find an approach that I'm aligned with."*

This is a common problem and one I've also struggled with. The answer lies in connecting deeply with your potential clients. It's much easier to sell in a genuine way when you care about the people you serve.

You want to make offers from the heart without using uncomfortable persuasion techniques. When you do this, the right people will want to work with you.

The other key is to practice making offers. Face your fear and gradually you will become more at ease with the process of selling. This is exactly what Pauline did.

Pauline set a goal to reach out to a handful of people every week. She asked if they knew anyone who might be interested in coaching with her. The more times she did this, the more comfortable she became with the process.

And of course, if you want to find paying clients you need to make offers. Pauline first started looking for clients in November of 2018. She had a deadline. She needed to find five paying clients before her coaching certification program started in January.

This deadline created a lot of pressure. Pauline said:

> *"I'm trying not to panic about my deadline to have five clients for my certification."*

She stuck with it, and over the next three months she signed not five, but six paying clients.

What do you think? Do you dream of starting a business but share many of the fears Pauline faced? Her story is a great reminder that you may start out with a business idea in mind, then discover the original idea no longer fits or isn't profitable. Changing tracks is more common than you might think. Often, it's only when we test our ideas that we discover whether they will work in the real world.

If you're an all-in type of person who likes to start immediately and figure it out as you go, you might feel frustrated by the idea of testing first. I encourage you to take time as you explore your business topics. Notice any frustrations as they come up. Understand that frustrations are just feelings and feelings pass. As you lean into the process I'm outlining in this book, you'll have confidence knowing you've put in the groundwork to set up a home business that has the best chance for success.

In the next chapter, we'll cover how to identify your customers and clearly outline the value you will offer them.

10

MAKE YOUR BUSINESS STAND OUT

Congratulations! If you've completed the action steps in chapter eight, you should now have a topic for your business.

Remember, there are three components to your business idea:

1. **Topic** – This is the field or broad subject matter of your business. For example: health and nutrition, basketball, online business, cooking.

2. **Customers** – These are the people your business serves. For example: new dads, recent college graduates, people with celiac disease.

3. **Offering** – This is how you serve your customers. For example: an online course, a one-on-one coaching program, physical products.

In chapter eight, you focused on the topic and started to think about your offering. In this chapter you will get clearer on who your customers are and what you offer them (how you'll make money).

We'll start by defining your value proposition.

What is a Value Proposition?

All businesses—whether you're a solo freelancer or a huge corporation—need a value proposition. Your value proposition tells people why they should do business with you rather than someone else.

A strong value proposition does four things:

1. It's clear.

2. It's credible.

3. It's appealing to a target audience.

4. It's unique.

Here are some example value propositions:

> *Netflix: "Unlimited movies, TV shows, and more. Watch anywhere. Cancel anytime."*

Netflix differentiates itself by the depth of its content (unlimited movies, TV shows, and more) and the ease of access (watch anywhere, cancel anytime). Their value proposition meets all four of the above criteria. It's clear, credible, appealing, and unique.

> *Patreon: "Create on your own terms."*

Patreon is a platform that allows fans or "patrons" to pay creators for their work. The company positions itself by targeting a specific niche (creators) and solving a painful problem this market has (earning recurring revenue from their creations).

> *Shopify: "With you from first sale to full scale."*

Finally, we have Shopify. In the crowded marketplace of e-commerce platforms, Shopify positions itself as a one-stop solution. Their goal is to make online selling accessible to everyone and to stay with their customers through start-up and growth.

Your WOW Statement

Okay, you're not a huge corporation with a dedicated marketing team. But that doesn't mean you can't define your own value proposition.

My version of a value proposition is called your WOW Statement. This is an approach I've been teaching for over five years. I've used it to help writers, freelancers, coaches, and other online business owners attract more customers and earn more money.

A WOW Statement helps you create something that fulfills a need for a target audience and in a way that's unique to you. WOW is an acronym which stands for:

Who: Your ideal audience.

Outcome: A positive outcome your audience wants.

Why: Why you are different from others in your field.

Your WOW Statement is used everywhere. In your offer descriptions, your website copy, the emails you write, and all online and offline promotions.

By defining your WOW Statement now (and don't worry, it's easy to do and you can also change it over time) you'll be setting yourself up for success. Most new business owners jump in with their business idea without taking time up-front to get clear about what their business does and for whom.

There are five steps to creating your WOW Statement:

Step One: Research your audience

Step Two: Define your Who

Step Three: Define your Outcome

Step Four: Define your Why

Step Five: Capture your WOW Statement

In the action steps below, I walk you through exactly how to do these steps and create a WOW Statement (value proposition) for your new business.

Research Your Target Audience

You're going to spend time researching your target audience. You want to get to know them and understand their deepest pains and secret dreams. Spend time discovering who they are, what they care about, and what they want.

You can do this research in several ways. The first method is to do online research. Read relevant forums, online groups, Q&A sites, and sites with reviews (Amazon, Udemy, etc.). Refer to the work you did in chapter eight and delve deeper into your research sources.

The second method is to talk directly to your target audience. Meet people for coffee and ask them about their life and challenges. Or if you can't meet in person, chat with them online or on the phone. When talking with people, ask open-ended questions. Your goal is to explore their urgent pains and secret hopes and dreams.

Note that people are best at answering two types of questions: questions about past behavior and questions requiring them to voice an opinion on something. Here are some examples of questions you can ask:

Can you tell me about the last time you experienced [the problem you will help with]?

How did it make you feel?

What specifically about [the problem] keeps you awake at night?

What, if anything, have you done to solve that problem?

What do you like or dislike about the solutions you've tried?

Many successful businesses solve a problem the owner personally experienced and overcame. This is the basis of my business. I worked for years to build a business so that I could stay home with my kids and make money, without feeling torn between the two. I understand my audience because I've been through their struggles, shared their dreams, and still do.

Having a deep empathy for the people you serve gives you greater satisfaction in your work and attracts more of the right kind of customers to your business.

Now, you don't have to solve a problem you've personally experienced. But you must have a deep understanding of your target audience.

Action Steps

1. Start by researching your audience using one or more of the methods described above.

2. Make sure you write everything down (either in an online document or on paper). Capture as much detail as possible, including the specific language your target audience uses.

> I want you to get into the head of your potential customers. The best marketing comes when you care deeply about the people you serve. Put yourself in their shoes and understand exactly how you can help them move past their difficulties or realize their dreams.

3. Now that you understand your potential customers, describe your audience as fully as possible (demographics, emotions, values, beliefs, occupations, learning style, opinions, and more). Enter your description in the workbook or your journal. This is your "who."

NOTE: Your target audience doesn't have to be defined by demographics. For example, it may be a single professional who feels stuck in the corporate world and yearns to create a lifestyle business that can be run from anywhere in the world.

4. Okay, so you know who you're serving in your business. But do you know what they want? It's time to define the Outcome part of your WOW Statement. Refer to your research and answer the following questions.

What are your audience's urgent pains?

What are your audience's secret hopes and dreams?

What is your audience's dream solution that she'd pay almost anything for?

5. Now take your above answers and describe the biggest result you can provide your audience. Be sure to define the deep-rooted benefits your target customer experiences. For example, if you help people improve their copywriting skills, focus your message around the desirable result. This may be a larger audience, more followers, or more sales. *A Step-By-Step Guide to Writing Copy That Sells* is more persuasive than *How to Improve Your Copywriting Skills.*

6. Finally, you want to add your own unique twist to your business. This is your secret sauce and how you will differentiate yourself from other people in the same space. It determines why someone should buy from you and not from someone else.

To define your why, you will want to leverage what makes you uniquely you. Refer to your answers from chapter six. If you haven't already done so, ask friends, family, and colleagues to answer the following questions about you. I know this can be uncomfortable, but I think you'll find the exercise worthwhile.

i. What three things make you memorable? For example, an unusual quirk, a unique experience, your background, a prior occupation, your hobbies, etc.

ii. What are your greatest talents? These are often things you've been good at since childhood or areas in which people seek out your help. It may be the same five skills you circled in step two of chapter four.

iii. What do other people in your business category do that you can do differently?

Take this information and describe why you're unique within your niche. This is your "why."

7. Now you can capture your WOW Statement as a whole. Review your answers above and combine them into one statement. If you're struggling to create your WOW Statement, try using the following format:

I help [your WHO] who struggle with [URGENT PAINS] and want to [SECRET DREAMS]. What makes my approach unique is that [your WHY]. Because of this, people I work with [your OUTCOME].

Here's an example (this is my WOW Statement for my Make Money From Home book series): I help people who want to make money from home doing what they love. What makes my approach unique is that I show people how to leverage their strengths and use systems to build a business without working 40 hours a week. Because of this, I help people create profitable and fulfilling businesses that don't suck up all their time.

8. Review your WOW Statement. Consider it from the perspective of your target audience. Make sure you can answer yes to the following:

I understand this (it's clear).

I believe this (it's credible).

This is something I want (it appeals to me).

I can't get this in the way you're going to deliver it anywhere else (it's unique).

When you're happy with it, capture your WOW Statement in the value proposition section of your 1-Page Home Biz Plan.

◆◆◆

How did you do with your WOW statement? Are you excited? Scared? That's great! Remember, you want to work on a business idea that both excites AND scares you (at least a little). If you're feeling both emotions, you're on the right track.

Your WOW statement is a great way to keep your purpose and customers at the front of your mind as you build your business. It also helps you avoid unnecessary distraction that can throw you off-course.

Now, I'd like to share with you Clare's inspirational story. Clare highlights how she changed the focus of her business by following the steps in this chapter—getting clear about who her customers were and how she wanted to help solve their problems.

11

CLARE'S SUCCESS STORY

Launching an Online Coaching Program to a Small Email List

This is a case study with one of my clients, Clare Nielsen. When we met, Clare already had a thriving personal training business. Her goal was to grow her income without working longer hours, so she decided to leverage her in-person business and create an online coaching program.

Clare achieved so much during our time working together. Here are a few highlights:

* Clare gained clarity on what was important to her.

* Created an exciting plan for her business going forward.

* Finally beat the overwhelm of having too much to do.

* No longer felt drained and had greater flexibility to work when and how she wanted.

* Launched to an email list of 153 people and signed up 11 people (exceeding her launch goal).

You can find out more about Clare's business on her website: fit4ever-more.co.uk

Keep reading to see how Clare's story unfolded.

Long Work Hours and Little Flexibility

Clare is a successful personal trainer from East Ayrshire in Scotland. She has been running her personal training business for over seven years, following a career in financial services.

Clare is a trainer, coach, massage therapist, writer, and counselor. And she absolutely loves what she does. But, early in 2019, she found herself working long hours and with limited flexibility. As a mom, she wanted more time with her family.

She needed to create flexibility in her life. She couldn't take on more clients because she had no more hours to give to individual coaching sessions. She wanted to explore her passion as a writer in her own time and in her own place. Her schedule was out of control and she had to turn clients away.

Clare decided the best way to achieve her goals was to expand the online side of her business and develop a group version of her successful training plan. However, she struggled to figure out the big picture.

What would her business look like? How many people would she work with? What kind of work was she meant to do? What would she find most fulfilling and profitable? Would clients see the same results without her standing there?

When we first discussed her goals, Clare told me:

> *"I keep tying myself in knots around my marketing and getting bogged down in high level decisions on what I want to do longer term.... There are so many things I need to do it has sent me in a spin."*

66

Doing Work That Is Meaningful

Clare felt overwhelmed and struggled to find clarity, so we began by diving deep into what she wanted most in her business. I gave her exercises to help her identify her biggest dreams and create a future vision for herself.

Here's what Clare told me after doing these exercises:

"So, it dawned on me that I have lost sight of what I enjoy and am good at. Plus, I am going to burn out soon if I keep going at this pace. I made the decision a while ago to stop doing any classes and to focus on a one-to-one or two-to-one training model. My reasoning was that I could work more intensely with individuals, work from home, and eliminate nighttime work.

"However, nearly five years down the line, I realize it's starting to feel draining, not stimulating. I have a loyal client base and have trained the same clients every week. I mix up their training and they are seeing great results, but I miss the challenge of working with new faces and the interaction that comes in a group setting. I have started a new class of six and am really enjoying it. I think what I need to do is deliver a group version of my starter plan. Then I can pivot that into an online/remote basis using all the same materials."

And so, Clare's vision for an online version of her business began to take shape. She discovered that she could leverage all the materials she already had for her in-person business and quickly create an online program that would meet her clients' needs.

Creating An Online Coaching Program

Now that Clare had a plan to move forward, she set to work. She impressed me with her determination and drive. However, there were some hiccups along the way. Like the time she told me:

"I find myself questioning whether I should have a rest and just chill. And who did I think would ever buy the course, anyway!"

These kinds of doubts are normal. We all experience them. Especially when creating something new outside our comfort zone. It's times like this when you need a community or support system, an accountability group or person who helps you stay the course.

Of course, Clare did keep going. In fact, she created her online program and launched in just two months. Her launch was simple. She shared her new program with her Facebook group, her email list, and her existing clients.

There were no fancy sales pages, and no time or money wasted implementing complex technology. She took her idea to market fast and her strategy paid off.

At launch, Clare had 156 email subscribers and she signed up 11 people to her online program. She offered it to her beta testers at a discounted price of 85 GBP (approximately $110). Next time around, Clare plans to charge almost double that number.

And the key to her success? Clare leveraged what she does best and kept things simple. This allowed her to launch fast and create something her audience wanted. Here's what she told me about her results:

"The big shift for me is that I got rid of all the noise. Over the last couple of years, I had joined various Facebook groups, listened to podcasts, etc. But all that did was distract me and make me feel as if should be doing things differently. Stripping it right back and working out what I want to be doing and getting on with it has been great. It feels like my business again and I am not wasting time changing everything around."

We All Need Accountability

Working with Clare and seeing her success has been immensely rewarding for me. We're now firm friends and I'm excited to see her next steps in her business. When I asked Clare what has been most helpful to her in being part of my program, she said:

"Accountability as always.... I feel as if you've given me gentle prods in the right direction. I think the challenge with working from home and by yourself is that it's really hard not having someone to bounce ideas off of. I have joined various other groups and memberships, but have now cancelled them all and cleared my social media feeds of what everyone else is doing. I feel so much better and focused on my own business. You have really helped with that, too—thank you!"

Building a profitable business isn't easy. We need people to encourage us to keep moving forward. Together, we all have a greater chance of success.

I hope you enjoyed reading Clare's story. Perhaps you can relate to the challenges of not having clarity, locked into a work pattern that isn't sustainable, and the feeling of overwhelm that comes when you try to make something work that no longer fits.

Just like Clare, the steps you're following in this book will help you find the clarity you need, work the hours that suit you, and create a business that is joyful and meaningful.

Next up, it's time for the rubber to meet the road. Let's test your business idea.

12

MAKE SURE YOUR IDEA WILL FLY

In chapter ten, you defined your WOW Statement or value proposition and became clear on who your customer is and what they want. Now, are you ready to test your idea in the real world? In this chapter, you'll define a simple offering and test your business idea.

Note for bloggers and authors: The process described in this chapter works best if you plan to offer a service or product. If your main goal is to build an audience before monetizing, or if you want to write a book and get more book sales, then keep an open mind as you read this chapter. Later, I discuss other ways to test your blog or book idea when starting out.

Be aware that having a large audience around your topic does not guarantee you'll make money. If you want to earn an income from home, then I recommend completing all the steps in this book before starting your blog.

> *The sooner you start putting offers out into the world, the sooner you will begin making money from home.*

Okay, let's dig in and create your first offering.

How To Define Your Test Offering

In the action steps, I ask you to brainstorm five to 10 products or services you can offer your target audience. I don't want you to over-think this step. You're looking for a Minimum Viable Offering (MVO), the smallest offering that will serve your target audience.

Your goal is to quickly test your business idea by discovering whether people will pay for solutions in this space.

Let's say your business topic is health and moms with young children are your audience. The biggest outcome your target audience wants might be to look and feel the way they did before they had kids without having to spend hours at the gym.

Here are some example MVOs in this niche:

- A downloadable eBook of easy exercises you can do at home and without equipment.
- A one-on-one personalized coaching program to help moms lose their first 10 pounds.
- A four-week workout plan for busy moms delivered by email.
- A downloadable eBook of 12 healthy, easy-to-cook recipes.

Once you've brainstormed some ideas, pick one to move forward with. Select one idea that fulfills the following criteria:

1. There's demand for the solution.
2. You have the resources and knowledge to provide the solution.
3. You are interested in providing the offering.
4. You can create a minimum version of the solution in less than two weeks.

Some people get stuck at the idea of creating something in less than two weeks, especially if they plan to offer a product and not a service. But you shouldn't build a complex solution at this stage. Instead, move through the testing phase as quickly as possible. Don't spend weeks or months designing something only to discover nobody will buy it.

If the thing you want to sell is too big to create quickly, you can still test your idea by pre-selling it or pre-launching. I'll explain these terms shortly. So, if you have an idea but you can't see a way to create it quickly, don't let this stop you from moving forward with it.

Freelancers, you may want to skip this step. If you plan to provide freelance writing or virtual assistant services, you can test your idea by applying directly to freelancing jobs published on public job boards. In which case, you don't need to create and market a specific offering.

Write A Sales Letter For Your Offering

Once you pick a test offering, write a sales letter for it. This exercise helps you refine your offering by clearly communicating the value to your potential customers.

Your goal here is to create a no-brainer offer. Something so good you know it will be irresistible to your target audience. An offer you are confident (even excited!) to share.

My favorite way to do this is by using the *60-Minute Naked Truth Salesletter Formula*[1] by Dean Jackson. This exercise works well because it pushes you to get your ideas down on paper fast.

Below are the steps to write your sales letter. As you write your letter, hold a clear image of your potential customer in your head. If you know someone in real life who fits your customer profile, think about that person. The best marketing happens when you truly care about your potential customers and understand their needs at a deep level.

1. Start with the purpose of your letter. "I'm writing to you because I want you to..." Insert the naked-truth reason you're writing, as if you're making your request known to a lamp Genie who could grant your wish, like, "Take out your credit card and pay me $39 for my new book called..."

2. Provide reasons you are writing to this specific person. "The reason I'm writing to you specifically is because I think you want..." And then list the reasons in bullet form, such as reason #1, reason #2, reason #3, and so on.

3. List the features and benefits of your product or offer. "Here is a list of what you get when you [buy my book]...." Again, use bullets. First list the feature followed by the benefit, such as "You get [feature], which means [benefit]." Write as many as you can drum up at this point.

4. List top 10 questions and/or objections. You can say, "If I were to guess the top 10 questions or objections you will have about buying my product today, they would be..." Follow that by another bulleted list of the top 10 most asked questions or most pressing concerns.

5. Provide answers to those questions or objections. "So here's how I would clear those up for you..." Same idea as point #4. List, in bullet form, the answers to each and every question or concern you've uncovered.

6. Explain the guarantee or how you are removing the risks. "I want you to be completely without risk, so here's my guarantee..." Then explain how your guarantee works, how it reduces or removes the risk from the purchase in their minds, and how to take advantage of it if they need to.

7. The most important part is the call to action. "It's really easy to get started. You just..." (whatever it is they must do, such as "click this button," "fill in this form," "call this phone number," "return this coupon," etc.). Provide the exact, step-by-step instructions on how they can take action.

8. The result of following the call to action. "Once you decide to get started, here's what will happen..." Describe what's going to happen once they begin. Educate them on how they will get their product, and how they will consume it. Tell them how to make the best use of their new purchase.

9. Add an element of scarcity or a sense of urgency. But only if this is REAL. I don't recommend using false scarcity tactics (for example, by saying the offer is expiring when in fact it is not). "You need to do this right now because..." Tell them why they need to take action today. Is there a limit or a deadline? What will be the consequences if they don't take action? What are the ultimate costs of not going ahead today?

10. Finally, include testimonials from satisfied customers. "Here's a list of people who have already [done this] and exactly what happened for them..." Add testimonials or case studies from other customers. Of course, I don't need to remind you they must be real and genuine.

Price Your Offer

Now, you want to set a price for your offering. Below, I walk you through a simple process I use to price all my new products and services. It's quick and should help you avoid pricing paralysis.

At this stage, you're checking to see whether there's a market for your idea. I recommend setting a "no brainer" price. This doesn't mean you will compete on price over the long-term. But for now, you need to find out whether people will pay for your idea. The following process will help you come up with your no-brainer price.

Start by imagining that you are your ideal customer. From the perspective of your ideal customer, eager for the solution you provide, ask yourself:

"What is it worth to have this problem solved?"

Answer with the first number that comes to mind and write it down. Don't overthink this step or waste time worrying about what other people charge. Simply focus on selecting a price that's consistent with the transformation you offer. Also, make sure the price you write down is a little outside your comfort zone.

Now, make sure your price is realistic. When testing an idea, it's important to set a price that will allow you to quickly find your first paying customers. Don't worry, when you've gained experience and testimonials, you can increase your rates.

Review the number you wrote down in light of the following:

* your business topic (what's normal in your niche)

* your background and experience

* the transformation you deliver

* what's included in your offer

Does the number feel realistic? Will your ideal customer pay this price to work with you? If necessary, lower your price. But make sure your final number still makes you a tiny bit nervous. When someone pays you that magic number, you'll push yourself to provide massive results. And massive results make for happy customers, glowing testimonials, and repeat clients.

> *This new number is your target price. It is not your no-brainer price. This is the price you eventually plan to set for your offer.*

To turn your target price into a no-brainer price, you want to discount it by anywhere between 50 and 75 percent.

How To Test Your Offer

Okay, take a deep breath. It's time go out and present your offer to real people. There are many ways to do this. Below, I describe five places you can share your offer. But don't feel constrained by these. Use your imagination and be prepared to keep testing different ideas.

There are two steps to test your offer:

1. Show up and give value.

2. Tell people how you can help them.

When you give free value to people, you build trust and demonstrate your expertise. And when you do this, the value you put out into the world will eventually come back to you. Focus on serving people. Let go of your attachment to making money and commit to helping the people who need your solution.

Here are some ways you can show up and give value to people interested in your business topic:

1. Participate in forums and Facebook Groups related to your business topic. Answer questions and be a helpful and active member of the group.

2. Publish helpful posts on your social media profiles. Provide insight into your business topic and share your journey with people who follow you.

3. Attend in-person networking groups and connect with people. Look for ways you can give value and be of service to others in your local community.

4. Post long-form articles about your business topic on Medium. This is a free platform which has a built-in audience.

5. If you're a freelancer or virtual assistant, seek out job postings in your space and apply to them. You can find opportunities posted on Craigslist, Upwork, your local community, and online job boards.

Now, unless you're applying to published jobs, you may be wondering when and how to make offers to help people. After all, the goal here is to discover whether people will pay for your product or service.

Make offers as often as you can, but do so from a place of service and not from neediness or desperation. In other words, don't cold call people on their personal number or send them private messages asking to work with them. Instead, consistently share your offer in the same places in which you're already giving value.

Imagine you have the cure for cancer. You wouldn't send individual messages to people who may or may not need your help. You would shout about your cure from the rooftops. You would announce it to the world. Then you would wait for the people to come to you.

For example, if you're sharing your business journey on social media, you might post three or four times offering free value. Then, in every fifth post, tell people about your new product or service, but don't obsess over how often you post or the exact words you should use. Instead, believe you have something of value and can help people. Do this and customers will come to you without you chasing after them.

How To Evaluate Your Results

Building your business is an iterative process. Few entrepreneurs find success right out of the gate. You must test an idea, analyze your results, and then look for ways to improve. If you're prepared to keep testing and improving, then success is inevitable.

In the action steps, I ask you to make a commitment to show up and help people every day. Keep putting value out into the world and making offers to help people. Do this until you either have a paying customer or realize it's time to test a different idea.

Don't keep taking the same action if it isn't working. You must tweak your offer and what you're sharing based on feedback. This stage is all about discovery—figuring out what you want to do that people will also pay you for.

I suggest you evaluate your results at the end of every day. Or, if you can't manage daily, do so every time you make an offer. Write down your answers to the following questions:

1. What did I do? Write out the specific action steps you took.
2. What was the outcome of this action? Describe the results of your action. List the positive results first. Don't allow your brain to focus only on the undesirable outcomes. For example, number of people you engaged, number of inquiries or new clients, dollars earned, etc. Include numbers wherever possible.
3. How can I improve next time? Describe all the ways you think you might be able to improve on your results next time. For example, if you're a new coach, you could change how you describe your coaching offer, how often you post on social media, the number of offers you make, etc.

You must be prepared to keep testing and be open to failure. If you're willing to fail as many times as it takes, then success is guaranteed.

A Word About Fear

This is the hardest step in the process and it's normal to encounter some resistance at this point. In most cases, your hesitations are related to fear and uncertainty. It's scary putting yourself out there. Sharing your idea and asking for money is not always easy. Please trust in this process.

Feel the fear, don't fight it, and remember your feelings are normal. But don't give in to your doubts, either, and throw away all your hard work. This is an experiment. There's no such thing as failure. There's only feedback. You're simply putting something into the world to see how others respond. You can do this.

Now, there are some legitimate concerns you may have at this stage, so I want to address the most common ones.

Concern #1: How Do I find customers for something that doesn't exist yet?

If you plan to create a digital offering and it doesn't exist yet, you may be wondering how to find customers so you can test your idea. Here are some ways to test your idea even if you don't have a product yet:

1. Pre-sell your offering: Ask people to pay for your offer before you create it. This is the concept behind crowdfunding sites like Kickstarter and Indiegogo. Writers and creators can also use Patreon to find supporters who will pay for their creations. A previous client of mine even pre-sold her children's book with only a rough draft in her hand.

2. Launch your offering in beta mode: This is where you create a minimum version of your product. It's the first version that you intend to improve in the future. Ask people to buy the beta version of your product at a discounted price. For example, instead of creating a pre-recorded video course or membership site, you could deliver training via live workshops. These need minimum preparation and you can later turn the workshops into a digital product.

3. Pre-launch your offering: This is where you collect email addresses from people interested in your idea. It allows you to build an audience while you create your offer. It's a valid strategy, but less effective than collecting money for your idea. People give away their email address more easily than their cash.

By having a waitlist, you can see how many people are interested in your offer and get early feedback on what to include/leave out. You can create a waitlist between one and three months prior to your launch. Just make sure you keep in contact with people, so they don't lose interest before you launch.

Concern #2: I want to create a blog and build an audience First

You may also be a blogger and wondering how to look for paying customers when you don't have anything to sell. If you don't want to offer a paid service or product, I still recommend testing to find out whether an audience exists for your idea. Too many people put time and effort into creating a WordPress blog only to discover there's no viable audience for their topic. Here are two ways to test your topic and whether or not the topic has a passionate and engaged audience.

1. Start posting articles around your topic on Medium. The beauty of using Medium is that it's a free platform for writers. You can discover how much engagement and interest your writing garners without having to build a WordPress blog. You'll also discover how interested you are in writing about the topic. (Many bloggers get bored after their first month!)

2. Post articles around your topic on social media or in relevant forums. This is another free way to see if there's an engaged audience around your topic. Pick a platform where your target audience hangs out. Two popular options are Facebook and LinkedIn. Make sure you tailor your content to the platform. For example, a Facebook post is typically shorter than a full-length article. As with Medium, your goal is to establish whether or not a passionate and engaged audience exists around your topic.

Action Steps

1. Start by brainstorming potential products or services. You already started to do this in chapter ten. Now that you have more information about your audience's urgent pains and secret dreams, you will have some new ideas. Come up with five to 10 possible offerings.

2. Next, review your ideas against the list below. Pick one idea you're excited about that meets all the criteria:

- There's demand for the solution (e.g., people are already buying similar offerings).
- You have the resources and knowledge to provide the solution.
- You are interested in providing the offering.

- You can create a minimum version of the solution in less than two weeks.

3. Now, let's refine your offering by clearly communicating the value to your potential customers. The goal of this activity is to create a written description you can share with people. Follow the steps described earlier in this chapter and write your Naked Truth Salesletter.

4. Okay, you've defined your first offer and written a sales letter. You're missing one thing, and that's the price of your offer. Refer to *Price Your Offer* above and select a no-brainer price for your test offering. When you're done, fill out the "Offer" section inside your 1-Page Home Biz Plan.

5. Next, make a commitment to show up every day in at least one of the places described above in "How To Test Your Offer". Write out your commitment and share it with someone—an accountability partner, your spouse, a mastermind group.

6. Start showing up and putting value out into the world. Make sure you share something free more often than you make offers. Each time you share or connect with a person in real life, check in with yourself. Make sure you are coming from a place of service and not from an attachment to making money or landing the client.

7. Keep executing on your plan until you either have a paying customer or realize it's time to test a different idea. Make sure you keep tweaking your offer and what you're sharing based on feedback. Use the evaluation questions in this chapter to analyze your results. You can either do this every time you share an offer or (for maximum results) at the end of every day.

I've said it before, but it's worth repeating. Testing your idea is the hardest step in this book. Most of us experience deep uncertainty when it comes to sharing our ideas with others. And our doubts can escalate when asking people for money. I get it and ask you to stick with the process.

This is nothing more than an experiment. If your first offer isn't received well, iterate through the steps in this chapter again. Tweak or change your test offer and try a second time. You can do this.

◆◆◆

If you've completed the above steps and tested your offer, great work. This takes courage, patience and resilience. Make sure you celebrate your achievement even if your offer wasn't well received. You still showed up, did the work, and faced your fears.

> *Try to take a playful approach to this process, rather than seeing any setbacks as failures. Keep testing your ideas and offerings until you find the one that fits your audience.*

For further inspiration, read Kendra's success story on the next page. Kendra tested multiple business ideas before finding success. Her attempts included a snack vending machine business, an Amazon FBA private label business, an informational website with ads, print-on-demand e-commerce, and transcription editing work.

13

KENDRA'S SUCCESS STORY

Starting a Print-On-Demand Business for Passive Income

This is Kendra Scheesley's success story. Kendra has an e-commerce business, currently focused on Print-on-Demand (POD) physical products including mugs, wallets, tumblers, and other items.

My favorite thing about Kendra's story is her commitment to testing multiple business ideas and finding one that fits her life. As a busy mom, Kendra has little time to focus on her business. She needed to find a way to earn an income without trading her time for money.

Here are some of her highlights:

* Kendra tested multiple business models before landing on the perfect fit for her.

* Mastered many new skills including copywriting, building websites, accounting, product pricing, SEO, and paid advertising.

* Earned $4,000 from her POD business in one month.

* Created a net passive income between $150 and $1,000 (which is still growing).

You can find out more about Kendra's work-at-home adventures on her blog: discoverworkfromhome.com

Can you tell us a bit about yourself and your business?

I worked full-time for about 15 years in corporate IT as a programmer, business analyst, and project manager. It paid good money, but I always wanted more autonomy, flexibility, and income potential in my work. I saw running my own business as the way to do that, starting it as a side hustle and eventually making enough to quit my job.

I started my first side business in 2007 selling handmade jewelry. Over time I also tried a snack vending machine business, an Amazon FBA private label business, an informational website with ads, print-on-demand e-commerce, and transcription editing work.

Then, in 2017, I was laid off three weeks into my maternity leave. We had planned to put my daughter in daycare, but after she arrived it became important for me to take care of her while she was little.

I decided not to go back to corporate. Although my husband was able to take care of our financial obligations, I still wanted to bring in an income and have something to accomplish for myself. So, my side business became more of a focus.

How did you end up starting a Print-on-Demand business?

I found out about Print-on-Demand (POD) when an influencer I was following recommended a $297 course on how to do it.

POD is a business in which sales aren't limited by the hours you work or by the money you invest in inventory and advertising. The course was relatively inexpensive, and I've found that taking a course saves time and headache trying to figure it all out on my own.

I started my POD business at the end of 2016. I began with about 30 products, but then got off track. I found out I was pregnant in January 2017 and ended up focusing on my health and getting ready for the baby. During this time, I kept my products up and got one or two orders a month. This income was entirely passive.

When I was laid off, I considered several work-from-home options, including starting a blog, becoming a transcriptionist, virtual assistant, bookkeeper, and freelance writer.

I tried being a transcriptionist, but the hourly pay was too low for me and wouldn't bring any money in if I had to take a break for another maternity leave. That ultimately ruled out any kind of freelancing for me until we were done growing our family.

I started a blog about working from home, but I wanted evidence that I could make money. I felt this would give me more credibility and help me really make my blog a success.

That's when I looked at my POD business and realized it had already made enough to pay for the course. I decided POD would be a good place to focus my efforts.

What was the most challenging part as you got started?

Initially, it was easy for me to start a business. But over time, as various business models have not worked for me, I had to remind myself that I learned a lot from each experience. And that this knowledge will be a foundation for future success.

I know you need to keep trying things until you find the right fit. With Etsy, back in 2007, I learned how to set up and run a business. I didn't take a course on starting an Etsy business. I just did it. I learned how to take good photos, write engaging copy, do the accounting, price my products, do Etsy SEO, have good product constructions, source quality materials, test new offerings, ship products, and more. It was fun and I loved it. I overcame each new challenge by consistently working on incremental improvement.

How did you earn your first paycheck?

You never know where your first sale will come from, which is why it's so important to keep testing different things.

For example, my first Etsy sale was a trade with another seller. We bought each other's products so we could both get a review in our shops.

With Amazon private label, I got my first sales through Facebook Ads.

And with my current POD business, most of my traffic comes through organic Etsy and Amazon SEO. My first POD sale was a mug design in a niche I know well that doesn't have a lot available for buyers.

That first product sale design is still one of my bestsellers today.

Would you mind sharing how much you earn on average each month?

It varies because of retail seasonal trends. November and December show a huge jump in sales for the holiday gifting season, and then May/June also show a more modest jump for Mother's Day and Father's Day.

In the first eight months of focusing on POD, my monthly revenue varied from approximately $700 to $4,000. My net income (after expenses) was between $150 and $1,000.

Starting a Print-on-Demand business is a long-term commitment. The important thing to know about this business model is that it starts slow. However, it's not an hourly wage because I have it set up so it's mostly automated passive income. I continue growing the business by adding new POD products.

Can you tell us more about how you are growing your business?

I put up more designs every day. I add new product types from both existing and new production partners. For example, I started with mugs with one supplier and that's my main product. Since then, I've expanded to tumblers, shot glasses, wallets, and more, across five different suppliers.

When I get a good selling mug design, I order a case of it and have it shipped to Amazon to participate in their FBA program. I'm also experimenting with paid advertising on Amazon, Etsy, Google Shopping, Pinterest, and more.

What are you most looking forward to over the next year?

I'm looking forward to the 2019 gifting holiday season. I'll have a lot more products up as compared to last year's season.

I'm excited about beating my December 2018 record month of $4k in revenue.

Did you enjoy Kendra's story? What were your main takeaways? One important lesson is the importance of experimenting. Your first business idea may not be your best. And this is okay. As you test new ideas, you will learn skills and move closer to discovering the work you're meant to do.

So, once you have a business, what's next? In the following chapter, we'll talk about how to make your business official.

14

ORGANIZE THE LEGAL STUFF

Over the last few chapters, we've covered a lot of ground. By now, you should have developed and tested your business idea. This is a lot of work and you deserve to feel good about your progress.

Are you ready to make your business official? Please don't be put off by this step. Yes, there's some red tape involved, but it's not that difficult. Millions of small business owners and freelancers around the world have figured this stuff out, and you can, too.

In this chapter you will set up the legal and accounting side of your business.

> NOTE: The steps described here are specific to the U.S. If you live outside the U.S., check your local options. Also, I am not a lawyer. Always seek the appropriate legal advice for your business.

The Two Most Common Business Entities

You need to decide which type of business entity you'll use. A sole proprietorship is the most common business type, followed by a Limited Liability Company (LLC).

Being a sole proprietor means you're doing business, but you have not set up a formal business entity. It's the default business structure for a single-owner business. This type of business is not separate from the individual and no action is required to be a sole proprietor.

However, operating as a sole proprietor offers you no liability protection. This means if your business gets sued, your personal assets may be at risk. Although, you may be able to obtain business insurance to offset some of this liability.

LLC stands for Limited Liability Company. Owners of an LLC are called members and an LLC can have one, or many, members. LLCs with one owner are called single-member LLCs and when there is more than one owner, they're called multi-member LLCs. They are based on state law and formed at the state level.

One of the main reasons people start an LLC is for the liability protection. When you form an LLC, you are creating an entity separate from yourself (or other owners). Having liability protection means your personal assets are (generally) protected from any lawsuits, debts, or other liabilities.

When you form an LLC you need an Operating Agreement. Most states also require LLCs to renew annually and pay a fee. The due dates vary through the year depending on the state, so look up the requirement in your state. An annual report is usually a simple document noting any changes in the business.

LLCs should keep records of their business activities. It's also a good idea to hold at least an annual meeting and take minutes. If you're a single-member LLC, use this as an opportunity to get away to the coffee shop and have a meeting—even if it's just with yourself.

How To Form A Sole Proprietorship

To operate as a sole proprietor, there's nothing required other than to start doing business. As soon as you start a business, you become a sole proprietor.

As a sole proprietor, your business name is your name. If you want to call your business something else, you must file for an assumed name (doing business as, DBA) with your state.

You may also need licenses and/or permits depending on the type of business you have. If you're not sure, you can contact your Secretary of State's office and they will usually direct you to the right place.

You do not need a separate business tax ID number. You can use your social security number, but sole proprietors can file for a separate tax ID number if they want. This is called an Employer Identification Number (EIN).

You can file for an EIN online with the IRS.[1] Some people want to have an EIN so they don't have to share their social security number with the different entities they work with. If you have employees, you are required to have an EIN.

How To Form An LLC

To start an LLC, file formation documents with your state. These are usually called Articles of Organization. This requires a filing fee, which varies from state to state. A few states require you to publish "notice" that you are forming the LLC.

It's easy to form an LLC and it's something many people do on their own. Or, if you prefer, you can hire a lawyer to fill out the paperwork for you.

Single-member LLCs *can* use their social security number to do business, but I recommend obtaining a separate tax ID number (EIN). This shows you intend for the business to be separate from yourself and protects your social security number.

How Business Entities Are Taxed

Sole proprietorships and LLCs are generally taxed the same way. But LLCs can opt to be taxed as a corporation. Otherwise, both are taxed at the personal level. This means that any income you make from your business goes on your personal tax return on a Schedule C. Business expenses are also reported on your personal return.

It's important to keep track of all your expenses. We all have to pay taxes, but you don't want to pay more than you have to. I talk more about tracking your income and expenses below.

You will probably also be responsible for a Self-Employment tax. This covers Social Security and Medicare taxes. You can read more about that on the IRS site.[2] You may have to file these quarterly.

If you want to know more about business tax for your sole proprietorship or single-member LLC, check out the IRS's Self-Employed Individuals Tax Center.[3]

Select Your Business Entity

Now that you understand the two most popular business types when starting out, you want to select one that's best for you. Choosing the right business entity is an important part of starting your business on the right foot. But don't tie yourself in knots trying to decide what to do. You can always start out as a sole proprietor and then switch to an LLC when your income increases, or you see the need.

In deciding what to do, ask yourself:

1. How much do you want to manage as far as business formalities (filings, records, etc.)?

2. How much liability protection do you need for the type of business you have and what personal assets will you need to protect?

3. Are you prepared to pay the initial and ongoing filing fees for an LLC?

Some businesses can operate indefinitely as a sole proprietorship, or you may prefer the peace of mind that comes from forming an LLC.

Organize Your Finances

Besides legal, there are some financial considerations when running a business. You need to figure out how to handle bookkeeping and pay taxes.

Make sure you keep your business finances separate from your personal finances. I do this by using a separate business bank account. I also have a PayPal account that I use only for business purposes.

It took 30 minutes at my local bank to set up my business account. The account is free, though I have to keep a minimum balance to avoid charges. Your current bank will be happy to explain their business offerings, or you can shop around for a free account that meets your needs.

If you want to keep things simple, you can start out with just a PayPal account. I recommend getting a business PayPal account. If you're already a PayPal user, it's easy to upgrade from a personal account to a business account. Otherwise, visit PayPal's website and select the business option from the menu.

PayPal's business account includes several perks, such as better reporting and the ability to send invoices to your clients (e.g. if you're a coach or other service provider). It's free to set up. PayPal makes money by charging you a fee every time you receive a payment.

Remember to use your dedicated account(s) for all business-related income and expenses. This makes keeping detailed records much easier. Which brings us to the next topic—bookkeeping.

Manage Your Bookkeeping

Now, don't be put off by the idea of bookkeeping. It doesn't have to be complex. Bookkeeping is simply the act of recording every transaction for your business. You need to know who paid you, when they paid you, how much they paid you, and what they paid you for (and the same for expenses).

You can track your income and expenses in a variety of tools. Three free options are: an Excel spreadsheet, Mint and Wave (you can connect Mint and Wave to your business accounts and they will automatically import your business transactions). A popular paid service is FreshBooks.

Whatever system you use, make sure you keep your books up to date. If you do, tax time will be a breeze. We'll get to taxes in a moment. First, let's look at exactly what you need to track and how to do it.

Your income is what you get paid for your products or services. Your expenses are what you pay out to support your business. Allowable expenses vary depending on where you live and your local tax laws. Some possible business expenses are (make sure you always check the latest tax laws before claiming any expenses):

* Telephone and Internet service

* Books, magazines, reference materials

* Membership in professional organizations

* Equipment such as a laptop you use for your business

* Legal and professional fees

Make sure you keep all receipts. I have a folder on my laptop for any electronic receipts and an envelope for physical receipts.

I do my bookkeeping once a month. The process is simple and takes less than 30 minutes. I import all business transactions for the prior month into my bookkeeping software and make sure everything has been correctly categorized. I also make sure I write a brief description of each transaction and have a corresponding receipt on file.

In the actions steps, I walk you through setting up your business bank account(s) and starting a bookkeeping system.

Paying Taxes

Nobody likes paying taxes, but it's a necessary step. If you follow my advice and keep records, then taxes are easy. You can either give your bookkeeping records to your tax advisor or fill out the required forms yourself.

It's a good idea to start setting aside a portion of your business income to plan for future taxes. You're going to owe taxes on your new income stream, and you have to pay both the employer and employee tax portions when you're self-employed in the U.S. I recommend setting aside 20 to 30 percent of your net income.

I use the term net income because your business expenses serve as a tax deduction. Different expenses are deducted differently, so bear in mind that it's not a straight dollar for dollar offset. Also, be aware that tax laws do change. Refer to the IRS website for up to date information on exactly which items can be deducted.

Feel free to consult with your accountant. I'm not a tax advisor and each person's situation is different.

One final note on U.S. taxes: Most freelancers and home business owners pay taxes every quarter. However, in your first year you probably won't need to do this. As you grow your business, be aware of when you need to start paying quarterly instead of annually. Otherwise you may be hit with penalties and interest.

Action Steps

1. First, decide what kind of legal entity you want starting out. I started as a sole proprietor and later switched to an LLC. Do what's right for your current situation. You can always change it later.

2. If you decide to form an LLC, research the requirements in your state and fill out the necessary paperwork. Or you can hire a lawyer to complete this step for you.

3. If you decide to operate as a sole proprietor, there are no additional

steps you need to take to start your business. However, you may want to consider creating a DBA and applying for an EIN.

4. Regardless of which entity you select, you should also check whether you need to apply for any local permits or licenses. For example, I live in San Jose and am required to apply for an annual business license with the city.

5. Set up a separate bank account for your business. I also recommend applying for a PayPal Business account.

6. Next, decide how you're going to track your income and expenses. You can choose among many options including Excel spreadsheet, Mint, Wave, and FreshBooks. Pick one that best suits your needs.

7. Finally, put a recurring appointment on your calendar to update your books. I do this once a month. It's a simple process of importing all my business transactions and making sure they've been correctly categorized. I also store any digital and physical receipts in a safe place.

You've now completed the legal and financial sides of starting your home business. It takes a little time in the beginning, but once you've set everything up correctly, it should be easy to keep a track of your business activities.

We're on the home stretch now. Coming up, we'll explore how to create your website or other platform to share your business with the world. You'll also learn how to create a marketing plan that connects to your audience.

You may be feeling fear or self-doubt at the thought of promoting your business. Remember to relax, breathe, and allow those feelings —just as you did when you tested your offering. You're doing great.

15

GROW YOUR BUSINESS

In the previous chapter, you learned about the legal side of your business and what type of business entity to set up before moving forward. You also learned the importance of using a bookkeeping system to record your business expenses as you go, which will make life easier when tax time rolls around.

Now we're going to look at something that can make those who aren't tech savvy a bit nervous: creating your first website. I understand your reluctance, but please don't let it stop your progress. I'll walk you through a few different options so you can choose what will suit your business best.

Do I Need A Website?

A website acts like a virtual office space or shopfront for your business. It provides a place to store information about your products or services so potential customers can see what your business is all about before deciding to purchase from or work with you.

Even if you're not planning to sell a product or offer a service yet, a website provides a space to introduce people to you—your ideas, brand, perspectives. It also allows them to connect with you.

With the rise of so many online businesses, customers are more selective than ever about who they choose to trust. You can build rapport and establish trust when you have a website that clearly shows who you are and how you serve your customers.

Create A Website With WordPress

WordPress is one of the most common website platforms. If you decide to build a WordPress website, then you have two options. WordPress.com is for those who prefer to have the technical side of things handled by someone else. There are free and paid versions of this platform. WordPress.org is the self-hosted version. Self-hosted simply means that you are responsible for the technical aspects of your blog. This includes setup, security, and ongoing maintenance. There are also monthly or yearly costs involved.

Many people prefer the self-hosted option because you get greater control over what happens on your website. Free blogging platforms have preexisting conditions you must abide by. You have to follow all the rules in the Terms of Service for your platform. For instance, there are strict rules concerning advertisements and sponsored content. If you violate these conditions, you risk losing your site.

Control isn't the only thing you gain by paying a little extra for a self-hosted blog. You also have more options. When you create your blog on a free platform, you can't install many popular plugins, themes, or widgets.

There's one more reason why you will eventually want to build a self-hosted blog. It gives you credibility. When you give out your domain name, it looks like this:

yourdomainname.com

If you run on a free platform, your domain looks like this:

yourdomainname.wordpress.com

If you want to create a self-hosted website on WordPress, I have created a blog post that walks you through the technical steps to set this up. You can view the post at: sallyannmiller.com/how-to-start-a-successful-blog

What If I Don't Want A Website?

Now, you may still be testing out your business idea. Perhaps you're not ready to buy a domain name and create a self-hosted website. One alternative to a WordPress website is to create an about.me page. It's simple, effective, and takes less than five minutes to do. It's an easy way to create an online presence when starting out. You can always upgrade to a self-hosted WordPress website at a later date.

About.me offers registered users a platform where they can create a single page personal website. You can view my about.me page at:

about.me/sallyannmiller

There's a free version and paid version (my page is created with the free version). On a free about.me page you can:

1. Upload your photo.
2. Write a biography describing who you are and what you do.
3. Have a call to action button that redirects people to an external website (see below for some ideas on how to use this button).
4. Link to other online platforms and profiles including Facebook, Instagram, Twitter, Pinterest, LinkedIn, YouTube, Medium, Fiverr, Etsy, and many more.

In the paid version, you can also connect a domain, capture leads, and review analytics data (such as page stats and video details). The Pro version is $8/month. You would also pay approximately $10/year to buy a domain (e.g. yourname.com).

I would not typically recommend the Pro version of about.me. Once you're ready to set up a full-featured website, you're better off setting up a self-hosted WordPress site for maximum flexibility. However, the free about.me page is by far the simplest way to quickly create your online presence when you're starting out.

The Spotlight Button in about.me appears at the top of your profile. It can be used in different ways depending on the type of business you have. Use your Spotlight Button to encourage page visitors to follow a call to action.

On the free version of about.me, you're limited to one action type, which is: "Get more visitors to another website." However, this is much more flexible than it first appears. Here are some ways to use the Spotlight button:

If you're an author, select "Read my book" and link to your Amazon book page.

If you're a consultant, coach, or freelancer, select "Hire me" and link to a third party site where you offer your services (such as coach.me, Fiverr, or clarity.fm).

If you're a consultant, coach, or freelancer, select "Schedule an appointment" and link to your scheduling service (I like the free version of Calendly).

If you're raising money on a site like Patreon or Kickstarter, select "Back my campaign" and link to your funding page.

There are many more ways you can use the Spotlight Button. The key is to decide what you most want people to do.

Setting Up Your Online Presence

Now that you've read about the options, you need to select the best one. This decision can stop some people from moving forward, so I recommend that you don't take too long choosing. Just pick one and go with it. You can always upgrade later.

In the action steps at the end of this chapter, you'll find links to help you set up your website.

Create Your Marketing Plan

You've defined your offer and you have an online presence (a website). Now, you want to get the word out about your business and engage people as they connect with you. These are the "Invite" and "Engage" sections of your 1-Page Home Biz Plan.

Previously, you tested your business idea by sharing it with people you know. But for most businesses, mining your network is not a sustainable marketing plan.

You need to decide how you will market your business to create an ongoing flow of new customers (and income).

Now, let's discuss:

1. Your free offer – why people first connect with you.

2. Your marketing channels – how people find you.

3. Your engagement strategy – how you stay in touch.

Your Free Offer

Your free offer is how you encourage potential customers to first connect with you. In the online business world, this is typically a freebie that you offer in exchange for an email address.

But creating a freebie isn't your only option. In fact, when starting out I recommend keeping your free offer as simple as possible. Your goal is to attract the right people (the people you want to serve in your business) and encourage them to connect with you.

Here are some ideas. They may not all work for you, but they are effective ways to connect with people when starting out:

A free download – If you don't have an account with a business email service provider such as ConvertKit or MailerLite, you can ask people to email you at your personal email address and then you can send them a free download.

A discovery or strategy call – If you're a coach or consultant, you can offer free "getting to know you" calls.

An online community – This could be a discussion forum or a Facebook group centered on your business topic. While these can be time-consuming to run, they are a great way to connect with potential customers, build trust, and learn how you can best serve them.

A local Meetup group – If you prefer to connect in person, you could start a local group. Meetup.com makes it easy to find people who are interested in your business topic and to organize events.

A free workshop – This could be held online or in your local community.

A free sample of your work – If you're a freelancer or other service provider, you can offer free consults or sample work products to show prospective clients the quality of your work.

In the action steps, I ask you to pick a free offer. Keep this simple to start with, but make sure it appeals to your target audience and relates directly to your paid offering.

Your Marketing Channels

This is how you get the word out about your free offer. There's no one marketing strategy that will guarantee your success. All the following methods take time before gaining traction, and some work better for different audiences.

As always, the key is to find the approach that works for you. Pick one marketing strategy and give it your full attention for several months. If you're not getting results, tweak your strategy or move on to the next one.

Below is an overview of the main marketing channels. In the action steps, I ask you to pick one or two channels to start with.

Your Personal Network

Don't underestimate the power of your personal network. These are the people who already know and trust you.

This is an especially powerful strategy if you're offering a service. When you have an existing connection (however tenuous) it's much easier to get someone to read your email or answer your phone call.

We talked about how to mine your network in chapter twelve when we discussed how to test your offer.

Social Media

Many bloggers and online business owners leverage the power of social media to build a large audience. However, be careful about spending too much time on social media. A large social media following doesn't always translate into more customers and a bigger income.

Research the different social media platforms to see where your audience is hanging out, then pick a platform and dive in.

Other People's Audiences

When you connect with other business owners, you can share your ideas with someone else's audience and then invite them back to your business. You can do this online by guest posting or by being interviewed on other people's podcasts.

Guest posting is when you write a post that someone else publishes on their blog. You will often be asked to include a bio at the end of your guest post, which gives you a chance to include a link back to your website.

You can also connect with other business owners in your local community.

Collaboration

As you make connections in your niche, you'll discover opportunities to collaborate with others. Collaboration is a wonderful way to support other business owners and spread your message to each other's audiences.

The key to a successful collaboration is to build relationships with people who have an audience like yours and who share your values. Then work together in a way that benefits everyone. For example, I've collaborated with other business owners by co-authoring books.

Always think about what the other person gains from the project. Never focus on your own needs. When you enter a relationship thinking about what you can give to someone else, you'll build strong connections much faster. And you will gain a reputation as someone who is worth connecting with.

Local Marketing

Marketing in your local community is an often-overlooked strategy. But when starting out, it can be much more powerful than trying to be noticed in the crowded online space.

When people meet you in person, it's easier to form a connection. Deidre Edwards, the author of *Toolkit for Wellness*, handed out book-marks to promote her new book. She carried the bookmarks with her at all times.

This strategy worked well because it was personal and gave people a tangible reminder to read her book. Think about how you can spread the word in your local community.

Other Marketing Channels

There are numerous other channels, though most are better suited to more established businesses.

For example, if you have a blog, pay attention to Search Engine Optimization (SEO). And if you publish a book on Amazon, then you need to understand how the Amazon search engine works.

You can also consider paid advertising. However, only pay for advertising once you know who your audience is and whether they'll buy your offer. If you start doing paid advertising too early, you risk spending thousands of dollars targeting the wrong people and getting zero return on your investment.

Facebook advertising is a popular form of paid advertising for online business owners. Other options include Pinterest advertising, Google AdWords, Amazon Marketing Services (for books and other Amazon products), and YouTube advertising.

In all cases, you must be clear on who you are targeting, what those people want, and how you are going to get a return on your ad expenditure.

Your Engagement Strategy

Finally, you want to consider how to engage people after they connect with you. Most online business owners emphasize the importance of building an email list. Email marketing is less about building a following and more about forming a relationship with people who have already discovered you.

But don't think you have to sign up with an email service provider and start an email list on day one. While it's advisable to get your email list going sooner rather than later, there are other ways to stay in touch with your audience in the early days.

For example, you can:

- Engage with people on social media
- Collect names and email addresses in an Excel spreadsheet and send out a monthly newsletter (make sure you always ask permission first and give people an opt-out option)

- Start a free Facebook group or other community
- Follow up with contacts once a month via phone (for example if you have a service business)
- Host monthly in-person meetups or workshops

Then, when you start an email list, you'll have already formed a relationship with people who are interested in your business. You can invite these people to join your email list and continue to engage with them over time.

Action Steps

1. If you want to create a self-hosted website, go to www.wordpress.org and register for a website. You can also follow the steps in my blog post here: sallyannmiller.com/how-to-start-a-successful-blog

2. If you want to create a simple, one-page site, go to www.about.me and click the "Get your free page" button. Then create your about.me page.

3. Decide on your free offer. This is the offer you make to encourage people to connect with you and find out more about your services. This may be a free download, a discovery call, a free consultation, an online community, local meetup, workshops, and more. Enter your offer in the "Invite" section of your 1-Page Home Biz Plan.

4. Create a system to collect contact details from people who reach out to you. This may mean setting up an email list or you can simply start capturing email and phone details in a spreadsheet. Remember, you can always add a more sophisticated lead capture system later. Do what works best for you right now.

5. Next, pick one or two marketing channels and commit to these for the next three months. How are you going to keep getting the word out about your business so you have a constant stream of new customers or clients? Enter your marketing channels in the "Invite" section of your 1-Page Home Biz Plan.

6. Finally, decide how you want to engage people after they first connect with you. This is the "Engage" section of your 1-Page Home Biz Plan. At this stage of your business, don't be tempted to overcomplicate things. You goal is to form a tribe of people who resonate with your message. You want to demonstrate your expertise and build trust. And above all else, be human.

◆◆◆

Did you get your website or about.me page set up? If so, congratulations.

If not, I recommend you keep working on it until it's completed. If you're struggling, you can ask friends, family, or even your local library/neighborhood center to help you. There are also plenty of freelance web designers who provide this service if you are willing to pay.

> *Try not to get sucked into the thought that your website or page needs to be perfect before you can launch. Perfectionism is a mental roadblock that can throw even the most enthusiastic business owner off-track.*

If you're feeling this pressure, simply notice those thoughts when they pop up. And replace them with this thought: "Done is better than perfect." Remember, you can (and probably will) tweak your website as you learn more and grow in your business.

In the next chapter, you will learn how Stephanie Johnson used creative marketing strategies to sell her children's book, proving there's never just one way to do things.

16

STEPHANIE JOHNSON'S SUCCESS STORY

Creative Ways to Sell More Children's Books

S tephanie Johnson has an important message to share with the world and I've been honored to be a part of her journey. One of my favorite things about Stephanie's story is her creative approach to marketing her children's book. Her determination and confidence are an inspiration to any new business owner.

Here are some of Stephanie's highlights:

* She launched her business while staying home with two little ones.

* Pre-sold her first 50 books with only a rough draft in her hand.

* Sold over 700 copies of her children's book and earned $3,000 in one month.

* Started spreading a message she cares deeply about, one book at a time.

You can find Stephanie's book, *You Are... what will your child's inner narrative sound like?* on Amazon.

Can you tell us about yourself and your business?

Hi there! My name is Stephanie. I'm a work-at-home mom with two little ones.

My business is writing, illustrating, and marketing social-emotional children's books. My books teach children to look inside themselves for the strength and courage to thrive as the beautifully capable and uniquely talented individuals they are.

Why did you decide to start your business?

Two reasons, really—both are personal missions.

First, I want all children to hear simple, positive messaging from the people they look up to—starting at an early age, even before their reading skills have developed. All of us need genuine love, support, and encouragement so that we know and feel it and don't need to seek it externally. I'm fascinated by our inner narratives and how they help or hinder our everyday decisions both as children and as adults.

You know the saying, "Your thoughts become your words, actions, character, destiny…"? We have a gift as caretakers which is the ability to help shape our child's destiny. I started this business with a goal to help foster this gift.

My second reason is I want to support my family financially while not compromising my time with them. When writing children's books, every day can be take-your-child-to-work day! Staying home with my kids while earning an income is vital to me.

Was there anything holding you back from starting your business?

Is this a trick question? Ha! Yes, of course. Fear of the unknown, cash flow, time management—you name it.

There were many unknowns that I won't say held me back, but they certainly gave me pause. I was so naïve. I thought I could bring the story that lived in my mind and on my children's ears to every family with little cost and time. After all, the story was already written, right? How hard could it be?

After a year of hard work, late nights, and figuring things out, my book has finally been released. I became overwhelmed so many times in the beginning. Now, I'm very grateful to have my first book finished!

What was the most challenging part and how did you overcome it?

Without a doubt my biggest challenge was not knowing where to begin and finding so much information to sift through online. I ended up feeling lost, watching countless hours of tutorials.

That changed when I met Sally. It was like a weight was lifted off me. I had one place to find everything I needed to do pre-launch. I felt so clear knowing the action steps and when to do them. Sally's launch spreadsheet was a huge "ah-ha!" moment in my process.

How did you sell your first books?

I sold my first 50 books with only a rough draft of the book in hand to a local children's salon while my kids were getting haircuts. I booked another reading and author signing at a local kid's toy store with only the image on my phone of a cat looking at its lion reflection.

Both sales ended in tears—not mine, but the shop owners. This was my first YES and it felt incredible!

My third success happened when I saw the need for simple-to-read children's menus at local restaurants. Little kids order from pictures, not words they haven't learned to read yet. I asked a restaurant owner if I could use my brand logo on their menu in exchange for them selling my book at the cash register. I also offered to do the graphic design of a children's menu at no charge to help boost their family business.

The owner said yes right away.

Would you mind sharing how many books you've sold so far?

I launched less than a month ago and have sold over 700 books, earning just shy of $3,000. Most of this has been in person, plus some sales through Amazon's KDP platform.

My strategy is four-fold and evolving as I learn. First, every business I shop at (and love) is selling my book. I say something like:

> *"Hey, do you ever support local authors? This may be out of the blue, but I adore your shop. I'm a local author looking for ways to support local businesses and gain exposure to like-minded people. I could grab a copy of my book for you to look at and see if it would be a great fit for your clients. And if not, no biggie—you'll still see me in here every Tuesday."*

Then I quietly hand over my book. This has worked at hair salons, wildlife sanctuaries, and liquor stores. Everywhere I spend money.

Second, I'm contacting local and national news producers and influencers. I've found that mentioning, "I'm local and can be camera ready at your studio within an hour," is enticing. Particularly if you're an expert in your field and a spot opens up unexpectedly.

Third, I'm working to schedule an appearance at seminars where I can have direct contact with many people at one time.

The last strategy is asking for ideas from everyone I meet. People have been more supportive and insightful than I could've imagined. I had a colleague who said, "I know the contact at Chick-Fil-A corporate purchasing. Would you like me to introduce you?" Uhhhh, yes, please!

What are you most looking forward to over the next year?

I'm looking forward to my groundwork paying off. I'm confident that every action will cause a positive chain reaction...this ripple effect only grows with time.

Right now, I'm focused on daily actions that support the bigger picture. I'm creating a coloring book that will be cheaper to print than my children's color book. This will help me generate more revenue to grow my business more quickly.

I'm also visiting Ronald McDonald House this Mother's Day weekend to pay tribute to my late, younger brother (he's the cheetah in my book). I'll be donating books to every family at three different houses.

Finally, I'll be doing another big giveaway to Alex's Lemonade Stand at the July Northwestern Mutual Annual Meeting.

My kids join me on all these outings. And my biggest joy is that my young children are seeing Mommy doing work she believes in.

As Stephanie's story demonstrates, your marketing strategy is rarely fixed. It's a constantly evolving process that requires you to be creative and open-minded.

Just as Stephanie experienced, new ideas will often come to you as your business grows and develops. If you feel like you've run out of marketing ideas, you can always ask friends for tips. Inspiration can come from anywhere, even the most unlikely places.

By now, you should have completed all sections of your 1-Page Home Biz Plan except for the final "Measure" section. In the next chapter, I'll show you how to measure your progress to keep you on track and achieve your goal—building a profitable business.

17

BUILD A PROFITABLE BUSINESS

We're nearly done! In chapter fifteen, you learned the importance of creating an online presence. You also selected your free offer and worked out a marketing strategy for the next three months.

This is the final chapter, but it's an important one. You may be tempted to skip this section and not set up a tracking system. Please don't give in to the temptation. This step is key to building a profitable home business.

Let's dig in.

How To Track Your Progress

Tracking systems help you monitor your progress and observe the results of your actions. They show you what's helping you move toward your goal and what's not.

> *When what you're doing isn't getting you the results you want, it's time to try something different.*

To start tracking your progress, first identify which metrics relate directly to your main goal. For example, if you selected the Money Success Track, then you want to measure dollars earned each month (or week).

You can also track other metrics that drive earnings. Think about the measurable statistics that relate to your big goal. Some options are:

- Number of words or chapters written (for authors).
- Number of pitches sent (for freelancer writers).
- Number of offers made and number of new clients (for coaches).
- Page views (for bloggers).
- Unique visitors (for bloggers).
- Email subscribers (for online businesses).
- Products or services sold in numbers or dollars.
- Operating expenses (know how much you're spending, not just how much you're earning).
- Net income.

I don't recommend obsessing over numbers. There are many vanity metrics you can ignore. Remember, if it doesn't directly relate to your goal, then don't bother tracking it. Ask yourself, "Does this impact whether or not I'm achieving my main goal?"

Seth Godin, who is a well-respected thought leader in the entrepreneurial world, wrote the following on his blog:[1]

> The metaphor is pretty clear: more data isn't always better. In fact, in many cases, it's a costly distraction or even a chance to get the important stuff wrong.
>
> Here are the three principles:
>
> First, don't collect data unless it has a non-zero chance of changing your actions.
>
> Second, before you seek to collect data, consider the costs of processing that data.

Third, acknowledge that data collected isn't always accurate, and consider the costs of acting on data that's incorrect.

Once you have a handful of metrics to measure, set up a weekly or monthly review process. For example, you could block out 30 minutes on the first Monday of each month. In that time, update the numbers for the previous month and review any positive or negative changes.

Take note of any significant movements up or down and make sure you understand what's causing the fluctuations. This is how you know what's working and what's not working in your business.

For example, if the number of visits to your website jumps on a given day (once you've finished celebrating) look at your Google Analytics for that day. Do you know which blog post or website pages were visited? Where did the visitors come from? Did the traffic also result in a higher number of conversions (e.g. new product sales or email subscribers)?

Knowing this information will tell you what kind of content your readers enjoy, which marketing channels are working for you, and what blog posts or strategies are driving conversions (and ultimately dollars earned).

I track my metrics in an Excel spreadsheet and have a monthly meeting to review progress with my Virtual Assistant. This acts as an extra bit of accountability. Since I know we will be discussing our progress, I make sure to spend some time in advance updating and reviewing the numbers for the previous month.

Make Decisions And Act On Them

Now, some readers will set up a tracking system but then fail to act on the numbers. Looking at your spreadsheet each week or month does not create results in your business.

You must act on the feedback. Tweak your strategy. Try new tactics. Do more of what's driving the results you want. And stop doing what isn't.

One of the most important business skills you can learn is the ability to make decisions and act on them. Business is math. Either the numbers are moving in the desired direction or they are not. This sounds obvious, yet most new business owners fail to embrace this concept.

It can be easy to ignore the evidence when it isn't telling you what you want to hear. Don't fall into this trap. Analyze the data and find which areas of your business need improving. Don't let negative thoughts and feelings get in your way.

Keep trying new ideas and keep failing until you succeed. Do this over and again. Don't expect someone else to give you all the answers. Learn the skill of finding the answers on your own.

Are you gaining new followers? Are people buying from you? Are existing customers cancelling their accounts or failing to buy a second time? Find the weakest links in the chain and work to fix them.

This is the iterative process of building a business. Look at your data, make decisions, then follow through on your commitments. You don't need to read more books, take new courses, or learn a different set of tactics.

The answers aren't out there. They are right here inside you.

So, don't put the fate of your business into someone else's hands. They don't know you and your business like you do. You are the boss. And only you can make your business a success.

Action Steps

1. To start tracking your progress, first identify which metrics relate directly to your big goal. For example, if your goal is to earn $100,000,

then you want to measure dollars earned each month. You can also track other metrics that drive earnings. Think about what measurable statistics relate to the main goal of your blog. But don't try to track everything.

Enter the metrics you want to track in the "Metrics" section of your 1-Page Home Biz Plan. Also, add the metrics to your Success Tracker. This is where you will be capturing your progress each week or month.

2. Next, set up a weekly or monthly review process. Make sure you put dedicated time on your calendar to review your metrics on a regular basis.

3. Finally, act on the feedback from your tracking efforts. For example, every time I launch a new book on Amazon, I see a jump in sales and email sign-ups. But not all launches have the same effect. By studying the trends, I can see which books have the biggest impact. I can also see which marketing activities are most effective. This tells me the type of content my audience likes best and—more importantly—what I need to do to move closer to my goal of 100,000 book sales.

You've now completed the *Home Biz Planner* and set up all the systems you need to give your business the best chance at succeeding. It can be daunting to work out a marketing plan at first. But the effort you put in now will stop you from floundering as you engage with your potential customers.

Having a solid plan in place can also help prevent "shiny object syndrome," when you come across advertising for programs, tools, and strategies relating to business. In the online world, there is no shortage of distractions. I encourage you to keep coming back to the *Home Biz Planner* and your "why" any time you feel distracted or discouraged along the journey.

18

CONCLUSION

Y ou've reached the end of this book. I hope it's been a fun, inspiring, and challenging journey. How do you feel about your business idea now? Do you already have your first paying customer or client? If you're a blogger or writer, are people reading your work?

It's incredibly exciting to see your hard work paying off. Make sure you take the time to celebrate your wins along the way, even the small victories.

> *If you're still testing and tweaking your idea, don't worry. This is normal. It takes time to find the perfect business idea—one that fits you and your life.*

When I first started building my home business, there was so much to learn. I knew *why* I wanted to create a business that would be profitable without sacrificing precious time with my family. The *how* took a little longer to figure out.

By following the steps in this book, I've been able to successfully build, launch, and grow a thriving business on *my* terms. The people you have read about in this book have done the same. Now it's your turn.

Imagine what it would feel like to have your success story featured in a book or on a website. Imagine how satisfying it would be to create something of your own that is fulfilling, while still having time to spend with the people who matter the most. To pursue recreational activities that fill you up and energize you. To finally put a check mark next to your big dreams.

I've done it. I continue to do it. And I wrote this book to inspire people just like you to do the same.

At this point, I'd like you to think back to when you first picked up this book. If you've followed all the action steps, you have:

1. Committed to the process
2. Determined your "why"
3. Found accountability
4. Selected your success track
5. Set up your planning system
6. Created your *1-Page Biz Plan*
7. Brainstormed your business ideas
8. Explored your passions, skills, and interests
9. Designed the life you want
10. Selected your business idea
11. Created your offering
12. Tested your business idea
13. Decided on your business entity
14. Set up a bookkeeping system
15. Created your first website
16. Developed your marketing plan
17. Completed your *Home Biz Planner*
18. Established tracking system

Phew! That's a lot of action. You've covered so much ground and should be very proud of your results.

And if you're not seeing the results you hoped for, please don't panic. This is normal. Creating a business is all about experimentation. You try an idea, review your results, then either improve your idea or select a new one.

Try asking yourself the following questions. Do you need to pick another business idea to test? Can you pivot so that your idea is better aligned with who you are and what the market wants?

If you're not seeing measurable progress toward your next goal, you can also go back to chapter eight. Review the information and redo the action steps.

Set up the three systems we've covered in this book—your Weekly Priorities, Success Tracker, and 1-Page Home Biz Plan. These tools will help you create a profitable business without wasting time or chasing strategies that don't work.

Keep experimenting. And have FUN!

You may be tempted to dive into another book or course to continue this learning phase. It's easy to get stuck in the stage of information gathering, but this is simply a distraction that your brain uses to stop you from taking action.

As you systematically work through the activities in this book, you will see results. But I urge you to be patient. Don't feel like you must rush the process. If you take the time to create a strong foundation for your business, you'll avoid so many of the common obstacles that can knock you off-track.

Remember, building a successful home business won't happen overnight. Be gentle with yourself as you face new fears and over-come challenges along the way. Celebrate your wins. And keep working toward your goal.

You got this. You CAN build a profitable, fulfilling business.

If you enjoyed this book, check out the other titles in the Make Money From Home series at sallyannmiller.com/books

NOTES

7. Stephanie Donahue's Success Story

1. https://www.sallyannmiller.com/pursue-your-passion/
2. https://www.sallyannmiller.com/get-coaching-clients/

8. Find Your Business Idea

1. https://www.junglescout.com/estimator/

9. Pauline's Success Story

1. https://www.sallyannmiller.com/pursue-your-passion/

12. Make Sure Your Idea Will Fly

1. https://michelfortin.com/2009/06/09/dean-jacksons-60minute-naked-truth-salesletter-formula/%22%20%5Ct%20%22_blank

14. Organize The Legal Stuff

1. https://www.irs.gov/businesses/small-businesses-self-employed/apply-for-an-employer-identification-number-ein-online
2. https://www.irs.gov/businesses/small-businesses-self-employed/self-employ-ment-tax-social-security-and-medicare-taxes
3. https://www.irs.gov/businesses/small-businesses-self-employed/self-employed-individuals-tax-center

17. Build A Profitable Business

1. https://seths.blog/

ABOUT SALLY MILLER

Sally is a mom on a mission. She is passionate about answering the question, "Can modern moms have it all?" In a previous life, Sally worked for nineteen years as a project manager and business analyst in London and Silicon Valley. She has a Bachelor's Degree in Computer Science and a Master's Degree in Business Administration.

When her daughter was born, she discovered a new purpose. Sally left her corporate career to be a stay-at-home mom. She wanted to be a full-time mom to her kids. However, she missed the freedom and purpose that came from working. So Sally made a decision: She'd find a way to stay home with her kids and earn an income (without feeling torn between the two).

Sally is a self-confessed research geek and compulsive planner. She loves learning how stuff works, mastering new skills, and sharing her knowledge with others. Since leaving her nine-to-five, Sally has published ten books (and counting). She's also started multiple businesses and is committed to helping others like her earn an income from home.

You can find out more by visiting her website at: sallyannmiller.com

Made in the USA
Middletown, DE
28 July 2021

44994500R00076